MODELS OF THE UK ECONOMY

Models of the UK Economy

A Review by the ESRC Macroeconomic
Modelling Bureau

K. F. WALLIS (editor), M. J. ANDREWS, D. N. F. BELL,
P. G. FISHER and J. D. WHITLEY

OXFORD UNIVERSITY PRESS
1984

Oxford University Press, Walton Street, Oxford OX2 6DP

London New York Toronto
Delhi Bombay Calcutta Madras Karachi
Kuala Lumpur Singapore Hong Kong Tokyo
Nairobi Dar es Salaam Cape Town
Melbourne Auckland

and associated companies in
Beirut Berlin Ibadan Mexico City Nicosia

Oxford is a trade mark of Oxford University Press

Published in the United States
by Oxford University Press, New York

© ESRC Macroeconomic Modelling Bureau 1984

British Library Cataloguing in Publication Data

Models of the UK economy.
1. Great Britain—Economic conditions—1945-
—Mathematical models
I. Andrews, M.J.   II. Wallis, Kenneth F.
III. Macroeconomic Modelling Bureau
330.941'0858   HC256.6

ISBN 0-19-828501-9
ISBN 0-19-828503-3 Pbk.

Library of Congress Cataloging in Publication Data
Main entry under title:

Models of the UK economy.
Bibliography: p.
1. Great Britain—Economic policy—1945-
Mathematical models. 2. Economic forecasting—Great
Britain—Mathematical models. I. Wallis Kenneth Frank.
II. ESRC Macroeconomic Modelling Bureau.
III. Title: Models of the U.K. economy.
HC256.6.M63 1984   330.941'00724   84-20780

ISBN 0-19-828501-9
ISBN 0-19-828503-5 (pbk.)

Set by Grestun Graphics, Abingdon
Printed in Great Britain by
Biddles Ltd, Guildford, Surrey

Preface

The Social Science Research Council, now known as the Economic and Social Research Council, established the Macroeconomic Modelling Bureau at the University of Warwick in September 1983. The Council had been involved with macroeconomic modelling work almost since its foundation, through its support for the research directed by Professor Richard Stone at Cambridge; subsequently, various other groups had received its support. As there developed a number of different models, constructed for different purposes and in accordance with different views of the economy, the need also developed for a regular attempt to monitor, compare, and contrast their research output, and for improved accountability and accessibility. The Macroeconomic Modelling Bureau was set up in order to satisfy these demands.

This book is the first in a planned annual series of systematic appraisals of models and forecasts. Whereas the forecasts and associated policy prescriptions receive much public and professional attention, the reasons for divergences among them are not well understood, and the outside reader has little evidence on which to judge between competing claims. Through continuing analysis of model properties and forecast performance, and a gradual accumulation of studies of specific economic and statistical features, the series will contribute to the general understanding of models of the UK economy, and to the modelling process itself.

The Bureau's terms of reference cover the models of the ESRC-supported groups, together with the model of Her Majesty's Treasury and any other model whose deposit with the Bureau can be agreed. There are currently five models being developed with ESRC support: those of the Cambridge Growth Project (CGP), the City University Business School (CUBS), Liverpool University (LPL), the London Business School (LBS), and the National Institute of Economic and Social Research (NIESR). The first three are annual models, the last two quarterly. This book is concerned principally with these five models, all of which have been implemented at the University of Warwick Computer Unit, whence they are available to other academic researchers. Discussion of the Treasury model (HMT) is also included, but this is based on published sources and not on the authors' own computer-based analysis. Computer implementation of the models of the Treasury and the Bank of England is in progress.

Responsibility for the content, opinions, and conclusions of the book rests with the authors, comprising the Director and full-time research staff of the Bureau, and not with the Economic and Social Research Council. The authors are grateful for the co-operation of the modelling teams, the help and advice of the staff of the University of Warwick Computer Unit, the comments and suggestions of Marcus Miller and Mark Salmon, and the secretarial support and research assistance of Kerrie Beale and Carolyn Eaves.

Contents

List of Figures

List of Tables

Chapter 1

Introduction

1.1 Macroeconometric models

A macroeconometric model is a mathematical representation of the quantitative relationships among macroeconomic variables such as employment, national output, government expenditure, taxes, prices, interest rates, and exchange rates. Its equations comprise technical relations and accounting identities that reflect the national income accounting framework, and behavioural equations that describe the aggregate actions of consumers, producers, investors, financial institutions, and so forth. The numerical values of the parameters of behavioural relations are typically determined by statistical estimation from historical data, and the specification of such relations usually rests on a judicious blend of economic theory and statistical analysis. In addition to its use in forecasting and policy analysis, the model may also be used to test economic theories. Much attention is paid to dynamic aspects of the relations among variables, since the time form of the reaction of a target variable to a policy instrument is often as important as the overall magnitude of the reaction.

The construction of large-scale economy-wide models has developed over the last quarter of a century. The publication of quarterly data within a national income accounting framework was a prerequisite, and the first UK model was built in Oxford in the late 1950s (Klein *et al.*, 1961). Advances in econometric techniques and computer technology have facilitated a gradual increase in the size of models, and have also reduced the cost of model-building, hence the proliferation of models constructed for different purposes and in accordance with different views of the economy. The size of the larger models reflects their need to model the channels through which various policy instruments affect the economy, the number of available instruments in practice being large. Thus, the tax system involves a large number of different rates and allowances, and monetary and interest rate policy works through many channels. Study of the differential impact of specific measures on specific groups or sectors of the economy or on different categories of expenditure requires a complete account of these impacts.

Model-building is itself a dynamic process. Changes in legislative and institutional arrangements, developments in economic theory, the accumulation of new evidence, the re-interpretation of old evidence, analysis of forecast performance, and changes in policy objectives may all lead to changes in the specification of a model. Thus, in taking a snapshot at a particular point in time we run the risk of being out of date before we are in print. But the broad views taken by the modellers and their general philosophies change relatively slowly, and discussion of these approaches remains of value even though detailed specifications alter. And of course, charting these alterations is one of our longer-term objectives. Some groups have longer histories than others: whereas the London Business School has been publishing quarterly-model-based forecasts since 1966, the City University Business School model first saw the light of day in 1983. Since change is particularly rapid in the early life of a model, in this case there is an additional reason to expect some obsolescence in what follows.

In the remainder of this Introduction we provide the groundwork for the studies that follow in later chapters. First the econometric framework is set out, then an outline description of each model is given. There follow some notes on the practical implementation of these models and an overview of the subsequent chapters. Alternative introductions to some of these models and some of this material are given by Holden, Peel, and Thompson (1982) and Wallis (1979, Ch. IV). Reference should also be made to the volumes arising from the periodic conferences organized or supported by the Social Science Research Council. These contain, among other research papers, accounts of the development of various UK models, although standardized comparisons are usually absent. At the first such conference, held at Southampton in 1969 (Hilton and Heathfield, 1970), the papers on complete models were largely in the form of progress reports, but at a second conference, held at the London Business School three years later (Renton, 1975), it was possible for the first time to present detailed accounts of four UK models. A year later, in 1973, a further conference emphasized medium-term projections (Worswick and Blackaby, 1974). Next, in 1977 the Programme of Research in Econometric Methods at Imperial College organized a conference on recent developments in economic policy formulation through the use of macroeconomic models (Holly, Rustem, and Zarrop, 1979), and later that year a further meeting addressed the major policy issue of demand management through exercises conducted on three UK models (Posner, 1978). While these exercises took the models for granted and studied their policy implications, a second London Business School conference, in 1978, returned to an exploration of the models themselves and discussed technical aspects of model construction and use (Ormerod, 1979).

These six volumes represent a considerable research output, but the absence of systematic and consistent reporting on the relations between the models is notable, and is the reason for the preparation of this book.

1.2   Forecasting and policy analysis with an econometric model

In this section we provide a brief review of the relevant technical background. We first consider forecasting and dynamic analysis with a *linear* simultaneous equation model, reserving generalizations until later.

The model describes the relations between the elements of a vector of current endogenous variables y_t and a vector of predetermined (exogenous and lagged endogenous) variables z_t together with disturbances u_t, and is written in *structural form* as

$$By_t + Cz_t = u_t.$$

Estimates of the structural parameters B and C provide information about elasticities, marginal propensities, reaction coefficients, and so forth. Identities are distinguished as equations in which the numerical values of the parameters are given *a priori* and the disturbance term is identically zero. A normalization rule is needed, and this is usually implemented by assigning the value of 1 to the diagonal elements of B. Thus the ith equation might be considered to be the equation concerned primarily with the determination of the ith endogenous variable, but this interpretation is inappropriate given that all the y's are jointly dependent variables.

The contemporaneous feedbacks between endogenous variables are solved in the *reduced form*

$$y_t = \Pi z_t + v_t, \; \Pi = -B^{-1}C, v_t = B^{-1}u_t,$$

and these reduced-form equations can be used to forecast the endogenous variables one at a time. Having obtained estimates of the structural parameters, the reduced-form coefficient estimates may be calculated, and if the best forecasts of the disturbances are given by their mean values, namely zero, the forecasting equations are of the form

$$\hat{y}_t = \Pi z_t.$$

In *ex post* analysis, where the time subscript t refers to a period in the past, actual values of the predetermined variables are known; in *ex ante* exercises, corresponding to the usual forecasting problem where t refers to a future period, projected values of the predetermined variables must be supplied.

The use of a dynamic model to forecast over several time periods requires a distinction between exogenous and lagged endogenous variables, and so we partition z_t into a vector of purely exogenous variables x_t and the lagged endogenous variables y_{t-1}, taking a one-period lag without loss of generality. Partitioning the coefficient matrix to conform, the reduced form is now written

$$y_t = \Pi_1 y_{t-1} + \Pi_2 x_t + v_t.$$

Denoting the forecast origin by n ('now'), the one-step-ahead forecast is given as

$$\hat{y}_{n+1} = \Pi_1 y_n + \Pi_2 \hat{x}_{n+1}$$

where y_n are known values and $\hat{x}_{n+1}$ are projected values. Then, in calculating a sequence of forecasts up to some horizon h, the forecast for one period enters into the calculation of the next:

$$\hat{y}_{n+j} = \Pi_1 \hat{y}_{n+j-1} + \Pi_2 \hat{x}_{n+j}, \; j = 2, \ldots, h.$$

In practical forecasting, there are two important departures from this simple representation. First, most forecasters do not rely completely on their models to produce forecasts, but feel free to adjust them through a process known variously as 'residual adjustment', 'constant adjustment', or 'add factors'. Adjusting the constant term in an equation is equivalent to assigning a non-zero residual to the equation, and such adjustments might rest on the recent patterns of residuals, information about likely future developments not already incorporated in the model, or data revisions. At a simple level it might be ensured that the model is 'on track' in the current period by calculating the current residuals

$$\hat{v}_n = y_n - \hat{y}_n$$

and adding these back to give a sequence of adjusted forecasts

$$y^*_{n+j} = \Pi_1 y^*_{n+j-1} + \Pi_2 \hat{x}_{n+j} + \hat{v}_n, \quad j = 1, \ldots, h$$

which coincides with the actual data at the forecast origin. More generally, there is no presumption that the adjustments remain constant during the forecast period, and they are more commonly applied to structural equations, not reduced-form equations, in the face of the nonlinearity described below.

A second feature is that in practice there is not a clean break but a 'ragged edge' between the sample period for which data exist and the forecast period for which they do not, since official statistical agencies produce data at different intervals and with different delays. If the forecast origin, period n, is defined as the most recent period for which observations on all variables are available, then some data will usually be available for period $n + 1$; moreover, this period will usually be in the past, relative to the point in time at which the exercise is undertaken. Thus, the forecast exercise begins by forecasting the recent past. In the early stages of the forecast period that is relevant to this exercise, the values of some variables are already known, and for exogenous variables this simply reduces the extent of the required projections. For endogenous variables a common device is that of 'temporarily exogenizing' a variable whose value is known, by deleting it from the vector of endogenous variables for whose values the model is to be solved, and suppressing the corresponding structural equation. To the extent that the normalization rule is arbitrary, this temporary deletion also is arbitrary. An equivalent procedure, using the discussion of the previous paragraph, is to calculate and impose on the model solution the residual adjustment necessary to ensure that the adjusted forecast of the given variable(s) coincides with the observed value(s). Temporary exogeneity may also be used to accommodate announced policy regimes.

To analyse the dynamic properties of the model, we consider the time response of the endogenous variables to a unit step in an exogenous variable – the *dynamic multipliers*. A maintained change in an exogenous variable beginning at time t has continuing effects which work through the system as follows:

$$y_t \quad = \Pi_1 y_{t-1} + \Pi_2 x_t$$
$$y_{t+1} = \Pi_1 y_t + \Pi_2 x_{t+1} = \Pi_1^2 y_{t+1} + \Pi_2 x_{t+1} + \Pi_1 \Pi_2 x_t$$
$$y_{t+2} = \Pi_1 y_{t+1} + \Pi_2 x_{t+2} = \Pi_1^3 y_{t-1} + \Pi_2 x_{t+2} + \Pi_1 \Pi_2 x_{t+1} + \Pi_1^2 \Pi_2 x_t$$

and so on. Thus, the various *dynamic multipliers* are given by

Π_2 \hspace{2cm} impact multipliers

$\Pi_2 + \Pi_1\Pi_2$ \hspace{1.5cm} effect after one period

$(I + \Pi_1 + \Pi_1^2)\Pi_2$ \hspace{1cm} effect after two periods

$$(I + \Pi_1 + \ldots + \Pi_1^j)\Pi_2 \hspace{0.5cm} \text{effect after } j \text{ periods.}$$

If the model is stable, so that Π_1^j tends to a zero matrix as $j \to \infty$, then the long-run multipliers are given by

$$\sum_{j=0}^{\infty} \Pi_1^j \Pi_2 = (I - \Pi_1)^{-1}\Pi_2.$$

The (g, k) element of this matrix describes the change in the equilibrium or long-run level of the endogenous variable y_g in response to a unit change in the exogenous variable x_k. These quantities can be alternatively calculated by solving the implied relation among the static equilibrium values, namely

$$y^e = \Pi_1 y^e + \Pi_2 x^e$$

to obtain

$$y^e = (I - \Pi_1)^{-1}\Pi_2 x^e.$$

Dynamic multipliers describe the effects over time of an exogenous variable used as a policy instrument. In a linear model, the effect of a policy package can be evaluated by combining the appropriate multipliers. Alternatively, the effects of a policy can be studied by constructing a hypothetical or 'what-if' forecast from the model. The response of the economy to various policy scenarios may be estimated in this way, either as a counterfactual exercise over a historical period, or as an exercise over a future period under additional external assumptions. Optimal control techniques may also be used in policy analysis. An objective function is first specified, which is a scalar function of the values of the endogenous variables (targets) and policy instruments over the planning period. The optimal control problem is then to find the values of the policy instruments that, together with the resulting predicted values of the endogenous variables, maximize the objective function. The usefulness of these techniques in actual policy design requires agreement about the objective function, and a model that provides a good approximation to the structure of the economy. The techniques may be used to study the properties of a model, and also to evaluate past policies in the light of given objectives. Some optimal control exercises with UK models are reported in some of the conference proceedings referenced above, but the techniques are not used in the present volume.

A feature of some of the recent exercises on UK models is their use of the *rational expectations* hypothesis. The appearance of expectations of the future values of endogenous variables among the explanatory variables in behavioural equations is common, and often the unobserved expectations are assumed to be functions of the current and lagged values of a few observed variables, and so substituted out. If, instead, the expectations are assumed to be rational, in the sense of being the conditional expectations of the variables based on the model itself and on information up to the current period, then it is necessary to solve the model over a forecast period in an internally consistent manner. That is, the expectations variables appearing in the model coincide with the model's forecasts. A consistent expectations solution is a particular feature of the Liverpool model, discussed below, but has also been used in various exercises with other models.

Before going on to discuss the models, we note that the setting in which this technical background has been presented, namely that of a linear simultaneous equations model, is unrealistic, since the practical models are *nonlinear* in variables. Behavioural equations are often specified to be linear in the logarithms of variables, whereas identities relate the same variables linearly, and products and ratios of variables also appear as variables in their own right. The nonlinear system may be written in structural form as

$$f(y_t, z_t; \alpha) = u_t$$

where f is a vector of functions having as many elements as the vector y_t, and α is a vector of parameters. An explicit expression corresponding to the reduced form in the linear case does not exist, and solutions for the endogenous variables are obtained by numerical methods. Given values of the predetermined variables and parameters, forecasts $\hat{y}_t$ are typically obtained as the solutions, to any desired degree of accuracy, of the equations

$$f(\hat{y}_t, z_t; \alpha) = 0.$$

In nonlinear models this *deterministic* solution does not yield the conditional expectation of the endogenous variables, which may however be estimated by stochastic simulation methods. These methods are not usually employed in practical forecasting and policy analysis exercises, on grounds of computational cost. Fisher and Salmon (1984) present evidence on the nonlinear effects to be observed in two of the present models. Given a nonlinear model, the numerical implementation of the concepts presented above thus changes, and the linear algebra of reduced-form coefficients is no longer relevant; but the concepts remain unaltered. Dynamic multipliers still describe the time response of the endogenous variables to a unit change in an exogenous variable, but they are computed by comparing two model solution runs. First, a control solution or base run $\hat{y}_t$, $t = 1, \ldots, T$, is obtained over some historical or forecast period. Then the exogenous variable of interest, x_{kt}, say, is replaced by $x_{kt} + \delta$, and a new perturbed solution $\tilde{y}_t, t = 1, \ldots, T$, is obtained. The dynamic multipliers are then given as $(\tilde{y}_t - \hat{y}_t)/\delta$, $t = 1, \ldots T$. For a nonlinear model these multipliers may vary with the size of the perturbation δ, and may also depend on the particular exogenous variable settings in the base run; in practice, this does not seem to be a serious problem.

1.3 The UK models

This section gives a brief summary of the structure of the models used in later chapters. The emphasis is on the relations among economic variables represented by the structural form, and no attention is paid at this point to dynamic aspects of those relations. References to the more detailed accounts of the models are provided, and some of the main model characteristics are shown in Table 1.1. We first discuss the three quarterly models, then the three annual models.

London Business School (LBS)

The LBS model is an aggregate quarterly model covering 400 variables (just under 50 of which are exogenous) and with over 160 behavioural equations. It is based around the income–expenditure framework but is often referred to as an 'international monetarist' model. The model is set out fully in manuals produced regularly by the Centre for Economic Forecasting at LBS.

The determination of expenditures is based on the GDP accounting framework, as in other quarterly models. Consumer demand, fixed investment, stockbuilding, exports, and imports are determined endogenously, with government current expenditure predicted by a set of forecasting rules. While the model is similar to that of NIESR in that it is influenced largely by quantities rather than prices, prices do have a greater role than in the NIESR model. Inflation is generated via the interaction of wages, prices, and the exchange rate, with monetary growth having a direct effect on the exchange rate.

Consumer demand is split into durables and non-durables. The principal determinants of durables expenditure are real income, the minimum deposit rate, the real stock of liquid assets, the real interest rate, and the real stock of building society advances. Non-durables expenditure is explained by real income and the rate of inflation. Private non-oil fixed investment is determined endogenously and is split into two sectors: housing and non-housing. Housing investment is determined from a building society sub-sector using the availability of finance, real income, and interest rates, while output and a measure of velocity of money determine non-housing investment. Stockbuilding is split into manufacturing and distributive trades, with demand variables appearing in both equations and real interest rates in the former. Imports and exports are disaggregated. The major explanatory variables are world demand for exports and domestic demand for imports, with a competitiveness term (measured by relative labour costs) present in both cases.

The labour market consists of a set of employment equations and an equation relating the working population to the population of working age. In manufacturing, employment is explained by output, competitiveness, and the level of hours, and in the primary and tertiary sectors it is explained by the level of

Table 1.1   *Model characteristics*

Model	Wage formation	Price-setting	Inflation effect on expenditure	Interest rate effect on expenditure	Role of money supply	Financing assumption of fiscal policy	Role of fiscal policy	Role of expenditure	Exchange rate
LBS	Prices, labour taxes, consumption, output, interest rates	Cost mark-up	Negative, owing to real balance effects on private expenditure	Real rate affects consumption, stock-building, nominal rate effects, house building	Direct effect in fiscal investment: affects exchange rate			None	Oil effects, relative interest rates, relative money per unit of output, PSBR/GDP
NIESR	Real-wage target, unemployment, prices, hours	Cost mark-up plus pressure of demand effect	Inflation loss effect in consumption	Housing investment, inventories, real rate on consumption				In wage equation	Relative real interest rates, relative prices, current balance, oil reserves
HMT	Output, prices, labour taxes, public sector employment	Cost plus demand effects plus effect from competitors' prices	Inflation tax effect on consumption	Real interest rates affect consumption, stockbuilding; nominal rates affect investment	Direct effect on exchange rate	Can have fixed interest rates or fixed money target		In exchange rate equation	Relative money supply, real North Sea oil production, short-term increased interest rate differential
CGP	Exogenous	Cost mark-up	Real-wealth effect on consumption	Fixed investment	None			None	Exogenous

CUBS	Real wages	Monetary growth, output world trade, relative energy and material prices	None	Real money supply influences output; nominal money affects price level	Money growth fixed to 1986; then money and bonds grow in fixed proportion	Cannot affect aggregate demand but output can change through supply influences	None	Real rate determined by relative prices and oil effects
LPL	Real wages depend on unexpected inflation production, trade union membership, unemployment benefits, and employee taxes	Determined by supply of nominal money relative to demand for real balances	Inflation affects real financial wealth and hence expenditure	Nominal rates cause re-valuation of financial wealth; real rates affect substitution between real and financial assets	Direct effect on price expectations		All policy decisions fully anticipated	Immediate adjustment to relative price changes; real exchange rate is related to real wages

consumer demand, real interest rates, the female participation ratio, the change in unemployment, the population of working age, employer taxes, and the unemployment benefit ratio. Earnings depend on price inflation, output, the change in competitiveness, real interest rates, the real consumption wage, and the level of output.

The LBS model derives indices of producer output and input prices in the manufacturing sector, in addition to the customary final expenditure deflators which are necessary to produce current price estimates of final expenditure items. The producer output price is explained by a cost mark-up equation, and producer prices then enter into the consumer price equation along with unit labour costs and indirect taxes.

One of the distinctive features of the LBS model is the direct influence of money supply on the exchange rate through a term in the ratio of domestic to foreign money per unit of output. Other influences on the exchange rate are the level of domestic oil reserves, relative interest rates, the PSBR/GDP ratio, and the change in OPEC countries' balances. Relative prices or costs do not appear in this formulation.

Monetary growth is determined by a relationship that, like the exchange rate, depends on the PSBR/GDP ratio, the financial surplus of industrial and commercial companies, the cumulated PSBR, and nominal interest rates. Short-term interest rates are influenced primarily by world interest rates, with long rates related to short rates by a term structure equation (although these are primarily forecasting rules).

North Sea oil expenditures and incomes are distinguished, with the main effect of the variables on the remainder of the model being through the determination of government tax revenues.

National Institute of Economic and Social Research (NIESR)

The NIESR model is an aggregate quarterly model. There are almost 275 variables distinguished by the model, of which just over 100 are treated as exogenous, with some 90 behavioural equations. The version used is model 6.3, and a general description of model 6 is given by Britton (1983).

The model follows the Keynesian income–expenditure tradition. It can be viewed largely as a quantity adjustment model, being driven more by expenditures than by relative price factors.

The part of the model that can be viewed as the *IS* curve consists of relationships for consumer demand, fixed investment, stockbuilding, exports, and imports, with government expenditure exogenous. These items are largely demand-driven, although utilization enters into the determination of investment and relative prices influence exports and imports. The generation of inflation comes from the interaction of the wage, price, and exchange rate relationships, and inflation itself adversely affects consumer demand. Monetary factors have a minor role with some effects from interest rates on expenditure.

Consumer demand is disaggregated into durables and non-durables, with the main determinants being real income and the inflation loss on personal sector liquid assets. Fixed investment is split into six categories with three determined endogenously: housing, manufacturing, and non-manufacturing private. The housing sector is related to a building society sub-sector, and investment in private dwellings is related to interest rates, relative costs, and the availability of finance. The manufacturing equation is driven by lagged output and companies' cash flow, while non-manufacturing private investment is determined by consumer demand and capital stock. Stockbuilding in manufacturing is determined solely by lagged output, and in distributive trades by consumers' expenditure. The treatment of imports and exports is fairly standard with both variables disaggregated. Domestic activity and relative prices explain imports, and world demand and relative prices are the driving variables in the export equations.

The labour sector comprises a set of employment demand equations (where output is the sole variable for manufacturing and other private industries), an aggregate wage equation which includes terms in prices, a target real wage and unemployment, an hours equation, and a relationship to determine the level of unemployment from the labour force and employment.

Prices depend on unit import prices and unit labour costs with an allowance for indirect tax effects, and there is a demand pressure effect through the inclusion of a term in the change in manufacturing output. The exchange rate is determined by relative prices, the real value of domestic oil reserves, and the real value of the current account of the balance of payments. Real interest rate differentials also enter.

The measure of the broad money supply is explained by definitions relating the PSBR to the money stock, with bank-lending, debt sales, and currency transactions explained by behavioural equations with interest rates exogenous.

The NIESR model distinguishes a North Sea oil sector whose main role is to determine the government tax take through North Sea revenues, although the value of North Sea oil reserves also affects the exchange rate. Key variables in this sector are world oil prices, domestic oil output, and the exchange rate, with the first two being treated as predetermined.

Her Majesty's Treasury (HMT)

The Treasury model is the largest of the quarterly models. However, its size (700 equations and 1000 variables) reflects a detailed treatment of the public sector rather than theoretical complexity or empirical disaggregation. Our description relates to the public version of the HMT model made available in December 1983 and described by Barber (1984). This version is based on the 1980 constant-price National Accounts, although many of the equations have been re-scaled rather than re-estimated on the new data. Like the LBS model, the direct effect of money on the exchange rate introduces an influence of monetary factors in the inflation process.

Final expenditures are distinguished so as to satisfy the National Accounts income–expenditure identity. Consumption is separated into durables and non-durables. Consumer durables depend on real income, net financial wealth, and real interest rates. The income variable in the non-durables equation includes an adjustment for the effects of the inflation tax on real liquid assets. It also includes a net liquidity variable and terms in the nominal short interest rate and the rate of inflation.

Private non-residential fixed investment is disaggregated into manufacturing and non-manufacturing. The main activity variable is manufacturing output, with a separate role for capacity utilization. Output is also the main driving variable in the non-manufacturing equation, but here a capital stock variable is also included. Housing investment is related to relative prices and interest rates.

Public current and capital expenditure is largely exogenous. Stockbuilding is disaggregated by sector and asset and is determined principally by demand factors with real interest rates appearing in some of the relationships. The treatment of exports and imports is similar to that adopted in the LBS and NIESR models. Both exports and imports are diaggregated and depend on world and domestic demand respectively, and also on a measure of competitiveness based on relative costs.

The labour market consists of a set of employment and wage equations and a relationship to determine the level of registered unemployment from the exogenous labour force and employment. Employment depends solely on output, whereas wages depend on a variety of influences including output, prices, taxes, and public sector employment.

Prices are based on costs, with additional influences from capacity utilization, the level of activity, and competitors' prices. The exchange rate is determined by the expected future rate and the uncovered differential. The expected rate adjusts towards a long-run equilibrium which depends on relative money surplus, the real value of North Sea oil production, and the level of the short-term uncovered differential.

The monetary sector of the model calculates financial surpluses for four institutional sectors in order to produce net financial wealth. Total financial wealth is then allocated between sterling and foreign currency assets and finally between money, gilts, and other sterling assets. Thus, sterling M_3 ($£M_3$) is demand-determined and is dependent on gross domestic wealth, total fiscal expenditure, and interest rates. Short-term interest rates are all related to each other by simple mark-up relationships, with long rates related to short rates and to inflation expectations. The general level of interest rates can be either exogenous or endogenous if some aggregate measure of the money supply is fixed.

As in the LBS and NIESR models, the North Sea oil sector is modelled separately.

Cambridge Growth Project (CGP)

The CGP model is a structural Leontief input–output model embedded within a conventional macroeconomic model. The model is basically of the Keynesian type, emphasizing real flows rather than monetary or financial ones. Owing to the high degree of disaggregation (39 industries and commodities), the model is very detailed, with almost 5000 endogenous variables, 3000 exogenous variables, and around 16,000 behavioural parameters and coefficients. The model is annual, and the version described here corresponds to model MDM6. A basic reference is Barker (1976).

Like the three quarterly models, the CGP model determines expenditure and output using the framework of the GDP identity, but relationships are disaggregated into 39 commodities. Like the NIESR model, the CGP model is driven primarily by quantity factors rather than relative prices, with monetary factors having a minor influence. Whereas other models occasionally disaggregate, they usually do so only as a matter of convenience or necessity. In contrast, disaggregation in the CGP model is a methodological issue. This is not to say, however, that there are no aggregate relationships. Thus, there is an aggregate consumption equation, in which aggregate consumption is explained by transitory and permanent income and real wealth. There then follow disaggregated consumption relationships, the role of which is to allocate total consumption between individual commodities.

Private fixed investment is disaggregated by asset and industry. The main explanatory variables are gross output, interest rates, and the level of investment incentives. Stockbuilding is also disaggregated by asset and commodity, and explained by output.

The share of imports in the total supply of each commodity is determined by aggregate final demand and the relative price for each commodity. Exports are driven by relative prices and world demand.

The final demands for commodities obtained in this way are augmented by intermediate demands from the input–output matrix. These real demands are met by domestic output or imports.

The labour market consists of a set of employment and hours functions where industry output and the aggregate level of unemployment are the main explanatory factors for employment. In the forecasting version of the model, wages are exogenous.

Domestic prices are determined largely by a mark-up on costs, although for some industries the price of competing imports plays a role. The exchange rate is formally exogenous in the model.

As in the quarterly models, sectoral surpluses and deficits can be derived. The main difference is in the degree of disaggregation of the institutional sectors and the use of these surpluses/deficits to form a matrix of financial assets and liabilities which then determine the supply of money and external capital flows. Interest rates are assumed to be predetermined.

Along with most of the other models, the CGP model separately distinguishes the North Sea sector. It also has an energy sub-model; relations connected with energy demand are otherwise found only in the CUBS model.

City University Business School (CUBS)

The CUBS model is the newest of the UK macroeconomic models. It is a small annual model with just under 130 variables (of which 70 are exogenous) and has ten behavioural equations. A description of the model is given Beenstock *et al.* (1983).

The CUBS model differs from most of the other models in the absence of an income–expenditure framework and in its emphasis on supply-side factors in the determination of output. The model distinguishes four factors of production: capital, labour, energy, and raw materials. Demands for these factors are based on profit maximization within a perfectly competitive framework. Labour demand depends upon the real wage to employers, capital stock, and relative energy and materials prices. The labour market includes a formal labour supply schedule, unlike other models, and may or may not be market-clearing in that the actual real wage may not coincide with the equilibrium real wage. The analysis in Chapter 4 reveals that in practice the CUBS labour market is non-market-clearing. Labour supply depends on population and the real employee wage.

The factor demand equations and the assumed production function determine the supply of total private sector output for given factor prices and output price. A higher output price raises profits and factor demands, thus increasing production. The level of private sector output depends on the change in world trade, the change in the real money stock, the real exchange rate, inflation, energy demand, relative material prices, and the capital stock. Own-factor price effects are negative but cross-factor price effects can vary in sign. The overall price level is determined by aggregate supply and demand and is influenced mainly by monetary factors, but world trade and domestic output also have an influence. Thus, the supply curve is assumed to be vertical in the long run but aggregate demand can have a short-run influence. The real exchange rate is influenced by relative prices and the difference between the UK oil balance and that of other industrialized countries. The exchange rate balances the current and capital accounts of the balance of payments, which do not appear separately in the model.

There is no explicit modelling of the monetary sector. Official foreign exchange reserves are assumed to be exogenous, and a given PSBR is assumed to be financed by money or government debt.

Liverpool University Research Group in Macroeconomics (LPL)

The Liverpool model is a small annual model with less than 20 behavioural equations and with just over 50 variables in total (of which 20 are exogenous). It is 'new classical' in nature and is solved using a rational expectations algorithm which forces consistent expectations on the model. It is a monetarist model in the sense that higher monetary growth directly increases inflation with no role for cost factors. A general description is contained in Minford and Peel (1983). The present version, based on the 1980 constant-price National Accounts data, corresponds very closely to that described by Minford *et al.* (1984).

One of the main distinctions between the LPL model and other models is that private expenditure decisions are related to wealth and not income. Substitution between goods and financial assets is influenced by real interest rates. The budget surplus and balance of trade affect private financial holdings, with inflation reducing the real value of private money holdings and nominal interest rate changes altering the capital values of government debt and hence financial wealth.

The labour market is market-clearing by construction, with a demand function that contains real-wage and output variables and an unemployment/real-wage equation that depends on population, unemployment benefits, trade union membership, and expected inflation. The exchange rate responds immediately to relative price changes and to real wages, with an elasticity that reflects the labour share in total costs. Exports and imports are modelled jointly as a function of world trade, domestic income, and actual and expected real exchange rates. Inflation depends on the domestic money supply (which in turn is related to the PSBR/GDP ratio) and the demand for real-money balances.

As noted above, a key distinction in the LPL model is the use of consistent expectations; thus, such variables as expected future inflation or expected future exchange rates coincide with the model's forecasts of inflation or exchange rates respectively.

1.4 Implementation and overview

Model specifications are continuously changing, as already noted. In this section we record the details of the particular experimental design that underlies the exercises reported in later chapters, and provide a brief overview of those exercises.

The deposit of the models of the ESRC-supported teams with the Macroeconomic Modelling Bureau took place in late 1983–early 1984, when each group had just completed a forecasting round. The model version on which this forecast was based is the version used in our subsequent analysis. Details of the forecast database (exogenous variable projections), residual adjustments, temporary amendments, and so forth were also supplied, and replication of the published forecast from this information served as a check on our model implementation. The published forecasts/projections appeared as follows, with the indicated forecast horizon:

LBS	*Economic Outlook*, vol. 8, no. 1, October 1983	1987
NIESR	*National Institute Economic Review*, no. 106, November 1983	1985
CUBS	*Economic Review*, no. 2, Autumn 1983	1996
LPL	*Quarterly Economic Bulletin*, vol. 5, no. 1, March 1984	1997

Forecasts with the CGP model are prepared by Cambridge Econometrics Ltd, in this instance in July 1983 for the period 1984-90, and although not published were supplied to the Bureau.

In Chapter 2 we consider the overall properties of the models as revealed by dynamic multiplier analysis for a set of eight simulations. In each case the base run is the published forecast, and dynamic multipliers are calculated by comparing the base run with the alternative solution obtained by perturbing the relevant exogenous variable from its forecast database values. All other residual adjustments and exogeneity assumptions in the forecast are retained in both runs. Working with the forecast database gives a certain relevance to the results and allows one to consider the effect on the forecast of variations in assumptions, in a ready-reckoner fashion. Since the models are nonlinear, however, the multipliers may depend on the database. On the one hand, tests on the NIESR model using a historical database reveal little difference in simulation results. On the other hand, it is clear that the implied properties of the CUBS model are heavily influenced by a projected change in regime in 1986 concerning the financing of the PSBR; hence, as discussed in more detail below, these results must be treated with caution. Since no forecast assumptions are published by the Treasury, comparisons with the HMT model rest on the published results of simulations around an unpublished base run.

The actual forecasts are analysed in Chapter 3, which addresses the question of whether forecasts differ and, if so, how and why. By recomputing the forecasts under different exogenous assumptions, the impact of a particular team's assumptions can be assessed. Likewise, by varying residual adjustments, the contribution to the forecast of the forecaster's judgement, as reflected in these adjustments, can be assessed. A similar exercise was recently conducted on forecasts from some of these models by Artis (1982), who analysed material supplied by the model teams in response to his requests. The subsequent deposit of models and databases at the Bureau enables a consistent treatment across models to be achieved. Appropriate archiving and the passage of time will enable an *ex post* analysis of these forecasts to be made at some future date.

In the final two chapters we turn from the analysis of the overall properties of models and forecasts to the study of specific sectors and features of the models. Chapter 4 deals with the labour market, and provides a review of the modelling of earnings and employment by the teams, in the light of the current state of applied labour economics. Chapter 5 is concerned with the treatment of monetary and fiscal policy in the models. It provides an analysis of the issues that arise in attempting to measure the 'stance' of policy, and of the policy questions that may or may not be addressed by the models.

Chapter 2

Comparative Model Properties

2.1 Introduction

In this chapter the overall properties of the models are studied through simulation exercises and dynamic multiplier analysis. These examine the sensitivity of the endogenous variables to changes in particular exogenous variables, allowing for all feedbacks, contemporaneous and lagged. Dynamic multipliers are usually distinguished from partial elasticities calculated from single equations, since other endogenous variables are now allowed to vary. They also differ from policy analysis or scenario setting where typically multiple exogenous changes are made. Thus these dynamic multipliers characterize the model as it stands, with no additional effects. In particular, changes in expectations arising from changes in policy variables are ignored, except in models such as LPL, where they are formally included in the system.

Our general approach is to construct a base run of the model, which in this exercise is the published forecast, then to perturb the appropriate exogenous variable by a given shock and to compute a new solution run. The effects of this shock are then derived by comparing the results of this simulation with the base run. Both solutions include all the residual adjustments and exogeneity assumptions in the published forecast.

The input shocks have been selected to represent magnitudes observed in the actual data, at least in annual terms. To the extent that the models can be regarded as linear, the results can be interpreted as ready reckoners. Thus, the effects of a decrease of 10 per cent in the rate of VAT can be calculated by changing the sign of the simulation results describing the impact of an increase of 10 per cent; or the results of a 10 per cent reduction in the standard rate of tax can be approximately estimated by doubling the effects shown in the 5 per cent case. Tests on two of the models (NIESR and CGP) suggest that the results can be used in a ready-reckoner sense. However, this is legitimate only in a neighbourhood in which the linear approximation holds. More generally, the model itself might be regarded as a valid approximation only over the range of its sample experience, and hence we emphasize the use of shocks equivalent to observed changes in the data. For example, it would be inappropriate to generalize the results from a 5 per cent reduction in the tax rate to a complete removal of income tax. Moreover, the simulations might then be regarded as introducing a new policy regime and thus might become subject to the Lucas critique.

In nonlinear models the simulation results may also depend on the values of the exogenous variables in the base run. Tests on the NIESR model using an historical database reveal little difference between the simulation results, but this result is not necessarily of general applicability. The choice of simulation period is important for the CUBS model, since the financing of the PSBR involves a switch in regime in 1986. This has a marked effect on the simulation properties of the CUBS model.

Differences in model size often reflect the policy objective of the model. Thus, the somewhat large size of the Treasury model reflects the need to model in a detailed way the accounts of the public sector, whereas the even larger CGP model was developed in order to stress the role of disaggregation. Other models such as CUBS and LPL are more concerned with broad aggregates, and a smaller, more compact, model is sufficient. In focusing on broad aggregates the fact that a larger model may provide more information on matters about which a smaller model has nothing to say is neglected.

This point also applies to the time dimension. Models aimed more specifically at explaining short-term fluctuations in output and employment may say very little of interest about medium-term developments, while models designed to focus on the latter may abstract from short-run changes. However, we make no major distinction between the quarterly and annual models. An input shock is imposed as an impact in the first period of the simulation, whether this refers to a quarterly or an annual observation; and in some of the simulations this may imply that the size of the impact shock is quite large for the quarterly models. The results themselves are expressed in annual terms in order not to distort the comparisons. A more general issue is whether the time horizon is sufficiently long to enable the models to settle down to a long-run path. In the LPL model terminal conditions are set which ensure that the long-run solution is reached by the end of the time horizon, and these dominate the behaviour of the model as it approaches the terminal year. Some conclusions on this point are given in Section 2.5.

Finally, comparisons may be hindered by differences in the exogenous variable sets between models. Most of the exogenous variables in the models relate to developments in the world economy and to the setting of domestic economic policy and are thus broadly consistent. The main differences concern the absence of any treatment of the oil sector and indirect taxes in the LPL model, and the exogenous treatment of wages and the exchange rate in the CGP model. Despite this broad agreement on the range of fiscal policy instruments available, the standard financing assumptions underlying fiscal policy differ considerably between the models, and in very few of the models are these financing arrangements easily modified to ensure a standard treatment. The multipliers relating to fiscal policy instruments described below therefore assume the existing financing mechanisms embodied in the respective models, and detailed discussion of these mechanisms is reserved for Chapter 5.

2.2   The simulation experiments

Eight simulations are conducted and compared across the models. Four of these cover areas of domestic policy; two cover world or external developments; and two examine the sensitivity of the models to the exchange rate and earnings variables. The simulations have been chosen to illustrate key issues in macro-economics and to reflect the response of the models to key variables.

The four policy simulations are:

(i)   a permanent increase of £200 million (1975 prices) in government cur-rent expenditure on goods and services per quarter (with an equivalent increase in 1980 prices), equally split (where appropriate) between procurement and employment expenditure: this shock is equivalent to an annual increase of a £2 billion per annum in 1983 prices or $3\frac{1}{4}$ per cent of the level of expenditure;

(ii) a permanent 5 per cent reduction in the standard rate of income tax (e.g., from 30 to 28.5 per cent);

(iii) a permanent 10 per cent increase in the rate of VAT (e.g., from 15 to 16.5 per cent);

(iv) a 10 per cent reduction in the rate of unemployment benefit.

The first three simulations facilitate a comparison of the relative effects of some of the main fiscal instruments, government expenditure, direct and indirect taxation. Although the fourth simulation can be conducted on only three of the models (LBS, CUBS, and LPL), it illustrates a controversial issue in macro-economic policy.

The two external shocks are:

(v)   a permanent 5 per cent increase in world demand: since there are no other impacts on world economy variables, this might be equally regarded as a shock to UK export demand;

(vi) a permanent 10 per cent increase in world oil prices.

The final two simulations consider the sensitivity of the models to the central exchange rate and earnings variables. Not only are these variables important within most of the models as part of the transmission mechanism of fiscal and monetary policy, but they represent key areas which have proved difficult to model adequately in the past.

(vii) a permanent 5 per cent increase in the exchange rate;

(viii) a permanent 10 per cent increase in average earnings.

In all cases where the perturbed variables are otherwise endogenous they are exogenized before being shocked. That is, the variables are set equal to their base solution values and the relevant behavioural equations are deleted from the model. This applies mainly to the earnings and exchange rate variables in all but the CGP model. The exercises then indicate the sensitivity of particular forecasts or simulations to these variables. They represent their effects in a ready-reckoner sense, rather than suggesting the likely impact of a shock to the variable, which would normally be incorporated as a residual shock to the relevant equation (as, for example, with an increase in the exchange rate owing to external confi-dence). Our treatment ensures that the variable remains permanently at its new level, whereas shocking the equation allows feedbacks from other factors to occur, so that the variable in question usually changes by a different amount from the original shock. The purpose of these simulations is to compare the effects of these variables on the rest of the model, and they should not be interpreted as the results of policy changes.

Our discussion of the results cannot do justice to the full range of information generated by the models. Attention is generally focused on major macroeconomic indicators, particularly output, unemployment, and inflation.

2.3   Simulation results

(i)   Increase in government expenditure

The increase in public expenditure is assumed to be financed according to the built-in assumption in each model, as noted above. Different possibilities are available in the HMT and LPL models. In the former, nominal interest rates can be held constant (money financing) or varied to accommodate a variety of monetary targets: here we consider the case in which £M_3 is the monetary target. In the LPL model, assuming a fixed PSBR/GDP ratio corresponds to a fixed nominal money stock, although the *real* money stock can change as a result of wealth and interest rate changes; the assumption of an accommodating PSBR/GDP ratio involves a mixture of bond and money finance. In the CUBS base run the money growth rate is exogenous up to 1986, so that bonds are the residual finance; after 1986 the money base is assumed to grow at a rate of 1.6 per cent per annum faster than bonds. In the NIESR model constant interest rates are assumed, implying that the increase in government expenditure is financed entirely by monetary expansion.

The effects on unemployment and prices for three models exhibiting more than a minor inflation response are shown in Figure 2.1; results for all models are given in Table 2.1. The NIESR simulation shows a movement from the south-east to the north-west and illustrates a large reduction in unemployment in relation to the higher rate of inflation. In contrast, the CUBS and LPL simulations show a steady movement from the south-west to the north-east, indicating substantial inflation effects over time with declining unemployment effects.

GDP multipliers, representing the increase in GDP in relation to the increase in the expenditure shock, are presented in Figure 2.2. For the quarterly models, the multiplier in the LBS model rises gradually while those for the NIESR and HMT (fixed interest rate case) peak after two years and then decline, with the NIESR multiplier remaining above unity. The multipliers for the CGP and LPL models are consistently below unity.

The multiplier for the LPL model which incorporates a higher PSBR/GDP ratio is lower than for the non-accommodating case, while the HMT multiplier with a fixed money target falls continuously from a level of 0.77 in the first year to 0.26 in year 4. Comparing the fixed interest rate and fixed money simulations suggests a crowding-out effect of 25 per cent in the first year rising to over 70

Table 2.1 *Government expenditure simulation*

Shock £200 million (75 prices) per quarter or £400 million (80 prices) per quarter

Year	LBS	NIESR	HMT (a)	HMT (b)	CGP	CUBS	LPL (c)	(d)
GDP (% differences from base run)								
1	0.7	0.9	0.8	0.6	0.9	−0.1	1.1	0.8
2	0.7	1.0	0.9	0.5	0.9	−0.1	1.0	0.9
3	0.8	0.9	0.8	0.3	0.9	−0.1	0.9	0.8
4	0.8	0.8	0.7	0.2	0.9	0.2	0.9	0.7
5		0.8			0.9	0.2	0.9	0.6
6					0.9	0.2	0.9	0.6
7					0.8	0.2	0.8	0.6
8					0.8	0.1	0.8	0.5
13						0.2	0.7	0.5
Prices (% differences from base run)								
1	−0.13	–	0.3	0.3	–	–	−0.2	2.1
2	−0.20	0.50	0.9	0.6	−0.1	–	−0.4	4.2
3	−0.05	1.11	1.7	0.9	−0.1	–	−0.6	6.1
4		1.66	2.4	1.1	−0.1	0.7	−0.7	7.8
5		2.17			−0.1	1.9	−0.8	9.4
6					−0.1	3.8	−0.8	10.9
7					−0.1	6.0	−0.8	12.4
8					−0.1	8.3	−0.8	13.9
13						22.0	−0.8	22.3
Unemployment (differences from base run, thousands) *								
1	−153	−105			−145	−152	−96	−142
2	−143	−148			−146	−134	−120	−180
3	−142	−169			−147	−112	−114	−158
4	−149	−177			−148	−97	−99	−126
5		−178			−149	−76	−83	−94
6					−149	−58	−68	−71
7					−148	−45	−57	−54
8					−146	−37	−48	−42
13						−23	−26	−19

(a) fixed interest rate
(b) fixed money target
(c) non-accommodating PSBR/GDP ratio
(d) accommodating PSBR/GDP ratio
* no unemployment figures available for HMT

per cent in year 4, using the conventional measure of crowding out, namely $100\,(M-R)/M$, where M is the multiplier under accommodating money (fixed interest rates) and R is the multiplier under a fixed money target (bond finance).

It is apparent from Figure 2.2 that the multiplier from the CUBS model is significantly lower than from the other models (and indeed is negative for part

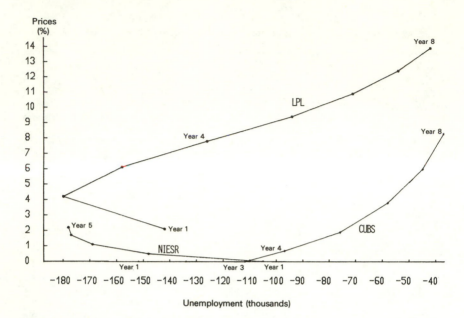

Fig. 2.1   Government expenditure shock: effects on unemployment and prices

of the period). This is a consequence of the lack of a relationship between public
sector employment and public sector output in the CUBS model. Since this
model does not have a national income identity but determines the level of
output directly, the implied increase in public sector output is not recorded.
Despite the very small output multiplier the reduction in unemployment in
the CUBS model in the first two years is no less than in most of the other
models.

The differences in GDP multipliers are not necessarily reflected in differences
in the level of unemployment, however (see Table 2.1). While CGP and the LPL
variable PSBR/GDP ratio simulations have relatively low multipliers, they have
unemployment effects in the short run comparable in magnitude to the models
possessing relatively high multipliers. Because of the different time dimensions
of the simulations, a proper comparison of the longer-run implications is not
possible. In contrast to the other models, unemployment effects diminish in the
CUBS, HMT, and LPL simulations as time passes, implying that the long-run
supply curve is more inelastic in these models.

Price effects are trivial in two cases: CGP and LBS. In the CGP case this
results from the assumption of exogenous wages. For LBS (where there is a small
fall in prices), the rising exchange rate counteracts any demand pressure on
prices. For Liverpool, under a fixed PSBR/GDP ratio, inflation is determined
largely by the fixed supply of money relative to the demand for real balances,
leading to a modest fall in prices.

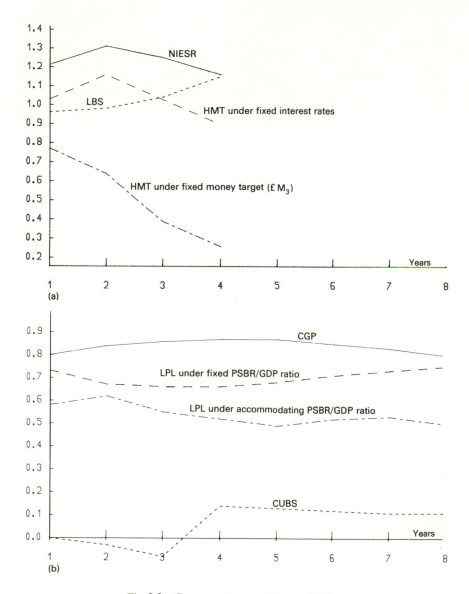

Fig. 2.2   Government expenditure multipliers

In the CUBS simulation there is no inflationary effect for the first three years. This is due to the fixed money growth rate in these years, and the CUBS simulation is therefore highly dependent on the choice of the period for analysing model properties. After 1986 (or from year 4), the rising money stock exerts a strong upward pressure on prices which are $8\frac{1}{4}$ per cent higher than in the published forecast after eight years. In the Liverpool case, where the PSBR/GDP ratio accommodates the higher level of public expenditure, this increases price expectations and inflation through an increase in money supply. Prices are $9\frac{1}{2}$ per cent higher after five years, by far the most inflationary response from the various simulations. Higher inflation in the NIESR simulation arises from a fall in the effective exchange rate, which in turn results from a decline in the current account of the balance of payments together with the effects of a loss in price competitiveness (as average earnings rise in response to the lower level of unemployment). The exchange rate mechanism is therefore of some importance, since it operates in a reverse direction in the LBS model, where a lower ratio of money per unit of output in the UK relative to the rest of the world causes an appreciation.

The HMT model, under fixed nominal interest rates, reveals a greater inflationary impact from increased government expenditure than NIESR and LBS. Nominal earnings rise more rapidly in the NIESR simulation than in the HMT case, despite the additional mechanism in the HMT earnings equation whereby higher public sector employment directly influences money earnings. The exchange rate falls a little more rapidly in the HMT model, leading to the greater price response. Under a fixed money target the inflation effect is more modest in the HMT model, as the exchange rate rises because of the higher level of interest rates. When the latter are held constant the exchange rate declines, and this is attributable to higher monetary growth.

The main demand effects accompanying the increased public sector demand are from consumption in both the NIESR and LBS models. Real income is boosted by higher employment and an improvement in real wages per head. The increase in consumption is higher for NIESR. This comes from the additional effect on export demand and hence employment as the exchange rate falls. The appreciating exchange rate in the LBS case results initially in lower export demand. As the price effects work their way through in the NIESR simulation the contribution from consumption fades, accompanied by lower investment, and is partially replaced by growing export demand. In the LBS simulation, consumption continues to be a major expansionary factor throughout. In the CGP model the higher public sector demand is supported by an increase in consumption demand.

A feature of the HMT demand effects is the inflation effect on consumption. While general inflation effects on consumption exist in most of the other models, there are two channels in the HMT consumption equation. First, inflation appears directly by influencing real interest rates. Second, the real income variable used in the consumption equation is adjusted for the 'inflation tax', that is, the loss in real value of liquid assets. The effects of higher inflation on savings behaviour depend on the balance between these effects. The inflation-tax effect plays an important role in reducing the impact on consumption demand as prices and nominal interest rates rise. Under a constant money target, the higher exchange rate results in a loss of competitiveness and lower export demand, and this is accompanied by higher interest rates which adversely affect private consumption.

In the LPL model, net exports worsen as a result of a higher real exchange rate when the PSBR/GDP ratio is fixed. The rise in the exchange rate comes about as a consequence of higher real wages following the initial reduction in unemployment. When the PSBR is allowed to rise to accommodate the higher level of government spending, the real exchange rate falls, reflecting higher inflation expectations and a fall in real wages. As the real wage adjustment is completed, the real exchange rate returns to equilibrium. However, the volume of net exports declines throughout as a consequence of higher income, although by a lesser extent than in the fixed PSBR/GDP case.

One important difference between the two LPL simulations is that the higher level of inflation in the accommodating PSBR case increases nominal interest rates, which together with inflation reduces the real value of privately held financial assets, leading to lower expenditure on goods. Whereas in the fixed PSBR/GDP case total wealth increases, leading to higher holdings of money and goods, there is now a fall in private sector wealth with consequent effects for holdings of money and goods. Another difference arising from the choice of financing assumption is that debt interest payments rise far more sharply when the PSBR/GDP ratio accommodates the higher level of public expenditure than when it does not.

As noted earlier, the increase in output in the CUBS model is understated since higher public expenditure does not affect aggregate supply. The main effects in the simulation come after 1986, when the money stock becomes endogenous. The consequent rise in money stock relative to the base forecast produces an upward pressure on prices and hence a lower output. The real wage and the real exchange rate remain unchanged throughout. If the money stock is permitted to be endogenous throughout some differences arise in the response of the CUBS model in this and other simulation experiments reported in this Chapter. However, these mostly concern the dynamics of adjustment rather than the long-run impact of the shock, many of the key variables approaching roughly the same level in 1996 whether money is treated as endogenous or exogenous in the period 1984–86.

The lower level of private sector output in the CUBS model is accompanied by lower private sector employment, reaching 120,000 after eight years. This therefore gradually crowds out the increase of 160,000–190,000 in public sector employment. In the CGP simulation private sector employment is also crowded out (to a lesser extent), but the mechanism here is different. The principal cause is the existence of marginal propensities to import of over 100 per cent for some industries, whereby a general increase in economic activity reduces some industrial outputs without altering the total demand for that commodity. In the LBS simulation the government sector provides the bulk of the additional employment, accounting for some 130,000 out of the 140,000–150,000 extra jobs. In the NIESR model, higher public sector employment accounts for between 50,000 and 60,000 extra jobs, with higher employment being generated principally in 'other' industries. Thus there is much variation between the models in the sectoral distribution of the increased employment resulting from higher government spending.

Total output is raised in all cases, but only in the NIESR and LBS models does higher public expenditure induce higher private expenditure, other than in the short run. In the other models private spending falls, the size of this effect clearly depending on the financing assumption. The trade-off between lower unemployment and higher inflation is clearly most favourable in the CGP model, and relatively more favourable in the LBS and NIESR models, than in the LPL or CUBS models.

Within the effects on total output there are some interesting compositional effects. In the LPL, NIESR, and LBS simulations net exports fall (although only temporarily in the case of NIESR), but spending on durable and non-durable goods rises in both the LPL and LBS simulations, whereas fixed investment falls in that of the NIESR.

(ii)   Reduction in income tax

We now turn to fiscal instruments aimed at the revenue side of the government's accounts, and in this simulation we reduce the standard rate of tax by 5 per cent (equivalent to $1\frac{1}{2}$ percentage points). In the case of the LPL model two variables are changed for this simulation: the overall tax rate variable and the variable which measures the average loss in tax and national insurance contributions experienced by employees.

Results are shown in Table 2.2. The output effects of this change are fairly small, with CGP and CUBS showing the greatest impact. LPL is the only model where the output effect is initially negative, and this is shown clearly in Figure 2.3, which presents the unemployment implications of the tax change. CUBS has the largest unemployment reduction in the short run, although this is reversed later on. The unemployment implications from the CGP, LBS, and NIESR simulations are quite similar in magnitude, with the LBS being the smallest. LBS, HMT, and NIESR produce a small increase in prices in contrast to the other models where prices fall (although this is later reversed in the CUBS simulation). The reduction in the CGP simulation occurs as a result of the fall in unit labour costs for a given wage rate and higher output level. A similar effect occurs in the public expenditure simulation.

A large contribution to the output effect in the NIESR model is from higher consumption arising from the improvement in real disposable income. The extra inflation resulting from higher demand lowers the exchange rate with a small beneficial effect from higher exports. However, there is a strong rise in imports so that the current balance of payments worsens. The LBS model gives very similar results. Comparable demand effects operate in the CGP model, but here there is an accelerator effect on fixed investment and a far stronger impact on real incomes and consumption. There is no retention ratio effect in the NIESR or LBS wage equations (see Chapter 4), so that the impact on wages is stronger than in the HMT model which includes such an effect. However, the effects of

Table 2.2 *Tax rate simulation*

5% reduction in standard rate of tax

Year	LBS	NIESR	HMT (a)	HMT (b)	CGP	CUBS	LPL
GDP (% differences from base run)							
1	0.1	0.1	0.2	0.1	0.5	0.1	−0.2
2	0.2	0.2	0.3	–	0.5	0.4	−0.1
3	0.3	0.2	0.3	0.1	0.5	0.6	−0.1
4	0.4	0.2	0.4	0.1	0.5	0.6	−0.1
5		0.2			0.4	0.5	–
6					0.4	0.4	0.1
7					0.4	0.4	0.1
8					0.3	0.4	0.2
13						0.5	0.2
Prices (% differences from base run)							
1	–	–	0.1	0.1	−0.2	–	−0.4
2	0.1	0.1	0.3	0.1	−0.3	−0.1	−1.0
3	0.2	0.1	0.5	−0.1	−0.3	−0.2	−1.5
4	0.2	0.2	0.8	−0.1	−0.3	−0.3	−1.9
5		0.2			−0.2	−0.2	−2.2
6					−0.2	0.2	−2.4
7					−0.1	0.8	−2.6
8					−0.1	1.6	−2.7
13						4.9	−2.8
Unemployment (differences from base run, thousands)							
1	−1	−9			−19	−59	27
2	−7	−20			−30	−148	26
3	−15	−27			−36	−161	17
4	−23	−33			−39	−111	8
5		−37			−40	−38	−1
6					−38	14	−8
7					−36	32	−11
8					−34	25	−13
13						1	−13

(*a*) fixed interest rate
(*b*) fixed money target

higher output outweigh the retention effect in the HMT model, so that earnings rise when interest rates are held constant; but with fixed money supply the retention ratio effect is the greater of the two influences. In the fixed interest rate case the main expansionary influence is private consumption, with exports reduced as a result of the lower exchange rate. With a fixed money target the output rise is considerably smaller, and the earnings effect (noted above), together with the rising exchange rate, leads to a fall in the price level after two years. The consumption effect is reduced and both real and nominal interest rates rise sharply.

In the LPL model a reduction in the tax rate requires a reduction in government spending to satisfy the required PSBR/GDP ratio. This largely explains the

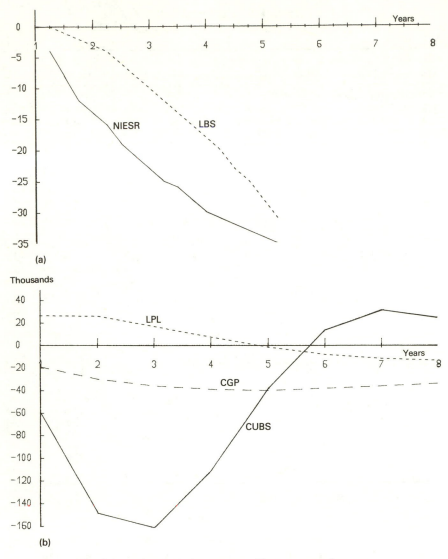

Fig. 2.3   Reduction in income tax: effects on unemployment

apparently 'perverse' initial decline in output and employment. Some of the impact of lower government spending on output is balanced by higher net exports (lower imports, owing to the fall in income) and higher financial wealth (from the small decrease in the budget deficit plus the trade gain), which in turn increases expenditure on goods. As the initial trade gains disappear, the lower level of government spending 'crowds in' an equivalent amount of private sector expenditure raising output and slightly lowering unemployment. With a fixed PSBR/GDP ratio there is a fall in prices reaching 2 per cent after five years.

As noted earlier, the CUBS model provides the most striking effects from a reduction in the tax rate. The lower tax rate leads to a reduction in real wages and raises labour supply. Total output rises throughout the simulation, and for the first four years of the simulation the price effects are minimal. The fall in real wages leads to higher labour demand and hence increased output, with the level of productivity falling for most of the simulation. As the longer-run effects on output from this source continue, labour supply rises, so offsetting some of the unemployment gains. After 1986 the switch to endogenous money determination gradually introduces an inflation effect, but it is the steady rise in labour supply that transforms initial reductions in unemployment into an increase. In the long run unemployment is unchanged, however.

One striking difference between the public expenditure simulation and that describing the impact of a lower tax rate is the smallness of the inflation effects in the latter. The output and unemployment effects are also lower. Note that the income tax and government expenditure shocks differ substantially in their direct impact on public finances. The government expenditure shock would directly increase the PSBR by £2 billion per annum at 1983 prices, whereas the tax shock would increase it by roughly half this amount. The *ex ante* balanced budget multiplier cannot be computed directly, but rough calculations of the *ex post* multiplier suggest positive values for CGP and NIESR and short-run positive effects for LBS. The results imply a more favourable outcome under public expenditure for LBS (lower prices and unemployment). However, it does appear that the improvement in unemployment under the public expenditure simulation for CGP and NIESR are large relative to the increase in inflation. One way of standardizing the comparison is to calculate the cost to the PSBR of each additional job under the various simulations. This is done in Section 2.4.

(iii)   Increase in the rate of VAT

Turning now to indirect taxation, we present the results of increasing the standard rate of VAT by 10 per cent, roughly equivalent to a $1\frac{1}{2}$ percentage point increase (Table 2.3). VAT, along with other indirect taxes, is not distinguished in the LPL model and no results are therefore given. A higher rate of VAT reduces the level of output and generally raises the price level. In the CUBS model, however, prices fall but there is negligible effect on output and unemployment. The rather surprising result in the CUBS simulation is that an increase in the rate of VAT lowers prices. This is because the higher indirect tax adjustment does not result in a higher market price index, yet the factor cost price index is derived by subtracting the new indirect tax adjustment from the (unchanged) value of the market price index. When money is allowed to be endogenous throughout this effect is dominated by the impact of higher monetary growth on the price level so that prices then rise throughout. In the LBS model unemployment falls despite lower output, owing to the fall in productivity. In the CGP model prices rise by about 1 per cent under the assumption that wages are fixed. This reduces real incomes and consumption and

Table 2.3   *VAT simulation*

10% increase in VAT rate

Year	LBS	NIESR	HMT (a)	HMT (b)	CGP	CUBS
GDP (% differences from base run)						
1	−0.1	−	−0.2	−0.2	−0.3	−
2	−0.2	−0.1	−0.5	−0.5	−0.4	−
3	−0.3	−0.2	−0.6	−0.5	−0.4	−
4	−0.4	−0.2	−0.6	−0.6	−0.4	−0.1
5		−0.2			−0.4	−0.1
6					−0.4	−0.1
7					−0.4	−0.1
8					−0.3	−0.1
13						−0.1
Prices (% differences from base run)						
1	0.2	0.2	0.6	0.9	0.8	−0.1
2	0.6	0.4	0.6	0.9	1.0	−0.1
3	1.0	0.5	0.5	0.8	1.0	−0.1
4	1.3	0.5	0.2	0.8	1.0	−0.2
5		0.5			1.0	−0.4
6					1.0	−0.6
7					1.0	−0.8
8					0.9	−1.1
13						−2.2
Unemployment (differences from base run, thousands)						
1	−1	4			15	−1
2	−8	10			24	−2
3	−12	19			30	−2
4	−5	27			34	−2
5					36	−2
6					36	−3
7					36	−3
8					34	−3
13						−

(a) fixed interest rate
(b) fixed money target

induces an investment slow-down. The net effect of a lower level of output and a small reduction in productivity is to increase unemployment by about 35,000. In the HMT model real earnings also fall, but the inflationary impact is eased by a rise in the exchange rate.

Real wages fall in the LBS model with earnings increasing by just 1 per cent after four years and prices by nearly $1\frac{1}{2}$ per cent. Real incomes and consumption therefore fall. The effect is initially to lower the exchange rate slightly, but to raise it in the longer run. Rising inflation leads to a cumulative consumption loss along with lower investment and export demand.

The NIESR model does not have an equivalent variable to the rate of VAT. Instead, the tax rate on consumers' expenditure is shocked by $3\frac{3}{4}$ per cent to give a roughly comparable tax revenue effect to the LBS simulation. In the NIESR model real wages are $\frac{1}{4}$ per cent lower than in the base run, leading to lower real income and consumption. However, fixed investment is the main source of lower demand.

The VAT shock illustrated here is equivalent to approximately one-and-a-half times the size of the income tax reduction in revenue terms. Apart from the case of CUBS, the inflation effects are stronger than for the income tax simulation and the unemployment effects weaker. The LPL model has nothing to say on this issue.

We are now in a position to draw together some of the results of the first three simulations. All the models show that an increase in government current expenditure on goods and services raises the total level of output in the economy and lowers the level of unemployment. In some of the models this is at the cost of higher inflation. Two of the models (NIESR and LBS) suggest that GDP increases by more than the initial injection of government expenditure; the remaining models imply some squeezing out of private sector demand. The models differ in the inflation cost of reducing unemployment (although the short-run unemployment effects themselves are very similar), with LPL (when the PSBR is raised to accommodate the increase) and CUBS implying the highest inflation cost and LPL (when the budget remains broadly balanced), LBS, and CGP the lowest cost. It is clear from the HMT results, however, that the budget financing assumption is critical in the assessment of the relative unemployment and inflation costs.

In the tax rate simulation the LPL model is the only model not to show an increase in output (since the PSBR is fixed). The output effects are generally of a lower order of magnitude than the equivalent government expenditure effects, however. Aside from LPL, all the models then show a reduction in unemployment in the short run, but the variation in the unemployment effect is greater than in the public expenditure simulation. Moreover, the reduction in unemployment in the CUBS model is reversed in the longer run. The inflation effects differ in direction between the models, with CUBS, CGP and LPL, and HMT (under a fixed money target) showing lower inflation and NIESR and LBS, higher inflation.

The results of the VAT simulation show a more uniform picture in terms of the effects on output. These are more pronounced for HMT than for the other models but are generally weaker than an equivalent change in taxation or government expenditure. The unemployment effects are correspondingly weak, although the productivity effect in the LBS model causes a fall in unemployment.

(iv) Reduction in unemployment benefits

The final policy simulation concerns a permanent 10 per cent reduction in the rate of unemployment benefits. The use of the benefit rate as a fiscal instrument is rather a recent development in macroeconomic models and has proved highly controversial. Three models (LBS, CUBS, and LPL) allow for an effect of un-employment benefits in the labour market (see Chapter 4), although NIESR finds no evidence for its inclusion. The results are shown in Table 2.4.

Table 2.4   *Unemployment benefit simulation*
10% reduction in benefit

Year	LBS	CUBS	LPL
GDP (% differences from base run)			
1	−	0.5	1.7
2	−	2.2	2.0
3	0.1	3.5	2.1
4	0.2	1.3	2.2
5		0.9	2.3
6		0.3	2.3
7		−0.1	2.4
8		−0.3	2.4
13		−0.1	2.5
Prices (% differences from base run)			
1	−	−0.1	−1.0
2	0.3	−0.6	−1.8
3	0.6	−1.2	−2.4
4	1.0	−4.8	−2.8
5		−10.0	−3.1
6		−15.7	−3.4
7		−20.8	−3.7
8		−24.8	−3.9
13		−39.4	−4.0
Unemployment (differences from base run, thousands)			
1	−56	−534	−174
2	−125	−1055	−291
3	−159	−1203	−337
4	−172	−994	−342
5		−703	−320
6		−441	−287
7		−311	−255
8		−302	−230
13		−380	−152

All three models give large unemployment effects with the CUBS model giving the largest and LBS the smallest. Note that the assumption of an exogen-ously determined money supply in the period 1984-86 makes a substantial difference to the size of the response in the CUBS model, though not to its direction. With endogenous money, unemployment falls by a maximum of 530,000 in 1986 and by 183,000 in 1996. In contrast, when the money supply is exogenous in the early part of the simulation, unemployment falls by 1.2 million by 1986 and by 300,000 by 1996. A more rapid increase in real wages under an endogenous money supply regime is the main contributory factor to this marked contrast in behaviour. Returning to the exogenous money simu-lation, output rises considerably in the short run, but returns to its original level after six or seven years (although unemployment remains permanently lower). Output is some $2\frac{1}{4}$ per cent higher on average in the LPL model, but in contrast, the LBS output effects are minimal.

The main effects on unemployment in the LBS model (Figure 2.4a) come through a slightly higher working population (building up to 50,000) being

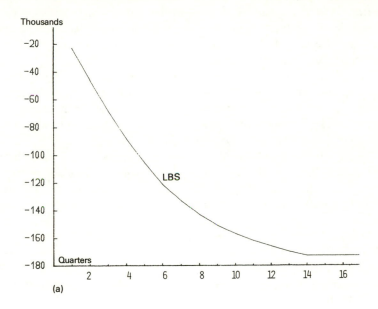

(a)

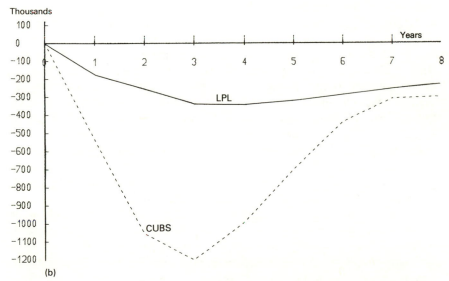

(b)

Fig. 2.4   Reduction in unemployment benefit rate: effects on unemployment

more than offset by higher employment in the primary and tertiary sectors — employment hardly changes in the other sectors of the economy. The small rise in inflation comes about as a result of higher wage costs per unit of output since demand and output are little changed.

In the CUBS model (Figure 2.4b) the fall in benefits shifts the labour supply curve to the right, leading to a fall in real wages and an increase in employment. The output effects originate from a fall in the real exchange rate and a rise in the growth of the real money stock, which result from the 5 per cent fall in real wages. The price effects are small until the money stock becomes endogenous after 1986, and then these effects cumulate.

In the LPL model lower benefits lower the equilibrium real wage and equilibrium unemployment. Actual real wages fall smoothly, reaching 2 per cent after five years. Lower inflation increases the real value of financial assets, and thereby spending on goods, while the lower exchange rate contributes towards the change in output through higher net exports.

While the three models considered here produce a reduction of between 150,000 and 300,000 in the level of unemployment in the medium term, the dynamic effects are quite different. The LPL model settles towards this level quite quickly, LBS moves smoothly, but CUBS produces a large interim decrease relating to the sharp change in real wages.

(v)   Increase in world trade

In this simulation, world demand is increased by 5 per cent in the first period of the simulation. Most of the world demand variables in the models refer to world trade, but the CGP model uses world production and the LBS model, both trade and production. Some of the differences in the results may then reflect a scaling problem since, for example, world production usually changes by a smaller proportion than world trade. In the LBS model the rest of the world economy variables are assumed to remain unchanged in the face of higher demand. This simulation thus represents a shock to UK export demand.

The domestic output effects (Table 2.5) are uniformly positive with the weakest effects occurring for CUBS and the strongest for LPL. Higher world demand leads to lower domestic prices for CGP and LPL but only indirectly for LBS and CUBS and to permanently higher prices for NIESR and HMT.

In the CGP model higher export demand is accompanied by an accelerator effect on investment and a smaller effect on consumption. Imports also rise quite strongly, however, so that the balance of payments gain amounts to £1 billion after four years and £$2\frac{1}{2}$ billion after eight years (see Figure 2.5).

The net export stimulus is greater in the LBS model, where the change in relative money per unit of output between the UK and the rest of the world produces a fall of around 1 per cent in the exchange rate. However, the consumption and investment effects are weaker than for the CGP simulation, and, moreover, investment falls from year 3, so that the domestic output effects weaken over time. Real wages rise by $\frac{1}{2}$ per cent by the second year of the

Table 2.5   *World demand simulation*

5% increase in world demand

Year	LBS	NIESR	HMT (a)	HMT (b)	CGP	CUBS	LPL
GDP (% differences from base run)							
1	0.6	0.5	0.8	0.7	0.8	0.7	1.5
2	0.7	0.5	1.0	0.8	0.9	−0.1	1.4
3	0.7	0.5	1.0	0.7	1.0	−	1.3
4	0.5	0.4	0.8	0.6	1.0	−	1.3
5		0.4			1.0	−	1.3
6					1.0	−	1.3
7					0.9	−	1.3
8					0.9	−	1.3
13						−	1.4
Prices (% differences from base run)							
1	−0.2	−	−	−	−0.2	−1.5	−0.4
2	−0.2	0.1	0.2	0.1	−0.4	−1.3	−0.7
3	0.1	0.3	0.6	0.2	−0.4	−0.5	−0.1
4	0.6	0.5	1.0	0.3	−0.4	0.1	−1.3
5		0.6			−0.4	0.3	−1.5
6					−0.4	0.2	−1.7
7					−0.3	0.1	−1.9
8					−0.3	−	−2.0
13						−	−2.2
Unemployment (differences from base run, thousands)							
1	−4	−30			−45	−12	−135
2	−13	−54			−81	5	−167
3	−33	−64			−109	2	−161
4	−52	−66			−121	1	−143
5		−65			−131	1	−122
6					−137	−	−102
7					−140	−	−87
8					−144	−	−76
13						−	−48

(*a*) fixed interest rate
(*b*) fixed money target

simulation and by 1 per cent after four years as improved trade competitiveness increases average earnings (see Chapter 4), while prices fall in the first two years. The balance of payments gain rises from £1½ billion in the first year to £2¾ billion after four years − considerably greater than the CGP result.

In contrast, higher world demand raises the exchange rate in the NIESR and HMT models. The GDP effect is greater in the latter than for the LBS (and NIESR), however, as the adverse effect of the higher exchange rate on net exports is more than compensated for by higher consumption demand. There is a fairly strong inflation effect in the HMT model resulting from higher earnings, with the real-wage earnings effect similar to that of LBS and larger than that of NIESR. The current account gain in the HMT model is just over

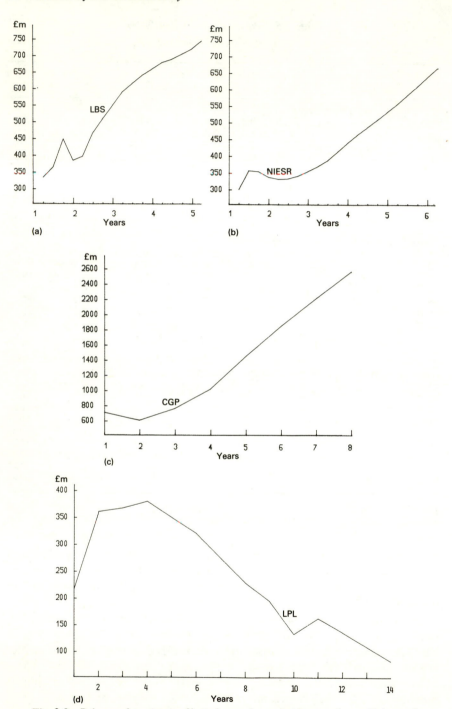

Fig. 2.5   Balance of payments effects from a 5 per cent increase in world demand

£1 billion for each of the first three years, rising to £1$\frac{3}{4}$ billion in the fourth year of the simulation, compared with £1.3 billion and £2 billion for the NIESR.

Lower price expectations in the LPL model result in an appreciation of the exchange rate which offsets some of the gain to net exports. The volume of government spending also rises as the budget deficit improves with a higher level of income, and the effects of a higher stock of financial assets (arising from the net inflow from abroad) induce higher spending on durable and non-durable goods. Gradually, however, the real exchange rate effect dominates the world demand on trade so that the volume of net exports declines. The higher level of equilibrium income lowers equilibrium unemployment by an amount similar to that experienced in the LBS and HMT cases.

The output gain is very short-lived in the CUBS model with the whole effect concentrated in the first year of the simulation.

The conclusion of this exercise is that higher world demand has its main impact on domestic output and unemployment with little impact on inflation. All the models show an improvement in output with the largest increase for LPL.

(vi)   Increase in the world price of oil

In this simulation we consider the effects of an external price shock by increasing the world price of oil by 10 per cent. The rest of the world environment is assumed to be unchanged. In the pre-North Sea oil era increases in the world price of oil were usually regarded as both deflationary and inflationary. The situation is now yet more complex, and this is revealed in the results of the simulations (see Table 2.6). Oil prices (or other world prices) do not appear in the LPL model, and a comparable simulation is not published by HMT, so this comparison covers four models.

The output effects are quite small for the CGP and NIESR models, slightly larger for LBS, and significantly larger for CUBS. The output effects are all adverse, while higher inflation results in the CGP and CUBS models, but not in the LBS and NIESR models. The output decline in the CUBS model comes about both as a result of a rise in the real exchange rate, with the relative trade balance in oil a direct influence, and as a consequence of lower energy demand. The general level of prices rises, even though the real exchange rate has appreciated owing to the direct impact of higher energy prices. Although the output loss remains fairly constant over time, the unemployment effect gradually disappears as the supply of labour diminishes.

In the NIESR model, although higher oil prices exert an upward pressure on prices of imports of goods, the average price of imports falls as the exchange rate appreciates in response to a higher value of oil reserves. This sets in motion a reduction in earnings and prices, with both 1 per cent lower after five years. The lower output is due to lower exports, in contrast to the CGP model, where lower real incomes and consumption are the main determinants of lower demand and output. Oil factors also lead to an appreciation of the exchange rate in the

Table 2.6   *Oil price simulation*

10% in increase in oil prices

Year	LBS	NIESR	CGP	CUBS
GDP (% differences from base run)				
1	−0.1	–	–	−0.7
2	−0.1	−0.1	–	−1.3
3	−0.1	−0.2	–	−1.2
4	−0.2	−0.2	−0.1	−1.1
5		−0.1	−0.1	−1.1
6			−0.1	−1.0
7			−0.1	−1.0
8			−0.1	−0.9
13				−1.0
Prices (% differences from base run)				
1	–	–	0.1	1.4
2	−1.1	−0.3	0.1	1.5
3	−2.4	−0.5	0.2	1.1
4	−4.4	−0.7	0.2	0.9
5		−0.9	0.2	1.0
6			0.2	1.4
7			0.2	1.8
8			0.2	2.0
13				4.2
Unemployment (differences from base run, thousands)				
1	−1	4	1	130
2	25	12	2	191
3	51	21	3	180
4	72	27	5	134
5		30	6	84
6			8	42
7			9	20
8			11	15
13				49

LBS model, but here the reduction in wages and prices is some 5 per cent after four years, the net export loss is less, and the consumption gain is greater than in the NIESR model, so that output does not fall by as much. However, productivity rises, so that the increase in unemployment is greater than for the NIESR case.

The results of the simulations show that an increase in the world price of oil does reduce the level of domestic output, but the effects are very small except in the CUBS model. Perhaps the most surprising result is that relating to the inflation effects, where the rise in oil prices leads to a reduction in domestic prices in the NIESR and LBS simulations. This effect emerges as a result of the inclusion of terms in the value of domestic oil reserves in the respective exchange rate equations, with a rise in world oil prices increasing the value of reserves and hence the exchange rate. This appreciation then outweighs the initial cost effects.

(vii)   Appreciation of the exchange rate

We now turn from domestic policy instruments and the world environment to the sensitivity of the models to two central variables. First we consider a 5 per cent permanent appreciation of the exchange rate. In the case of CUBS and LPL this relates to the real exchange rate (that is, the exchange rate adjusted for relative inflation in the UK and the rest of the world), but in the other models it relates to the nominal exchange rate. In all cases except CGP, where the exchange rate is already exogenous, the exchange rates are exogenized to their base solution values before being shocked. Results are given in Table 2.7.

Some of the implications for unemployment and prices are shown in Figure 2.6 with the balance of payments implications given in Figure 2.7. With the

Table 2.7   *Exchange rate simulation*

5% increase in exchange rate

Year	LBS	NIESR	HMT (a)	HMT (b)	CGP	CUBS	LPL
GDP (% differences from base run)							
1	−0.2	−0.1	−0.3	−0.1	−0.9	0.2	−1.1
2	−0.3	−0.2	−0.4	−0.1	−0.8	−	−0.8
3	−0.1	−0.1	−0.3	0.1	−0.8	0.9	−0.9
4	0.2	−0.1	−0.2	0.2	−0.8	0.6	−0.9
5		0.1			−0.8	0.6	−0.9
6					−0.8	0.6	−0.8
7					−0.9	0.6	−0.8
8					−0.9	0.5	−1.0
13						0.3	−1.3
Prices (% differences from base run)							
1	−0.6	−0.5	−2.0	−1.7	−0.6	−1.0	0.8
2	−1.5	−1.3	−2.8	−2.2	−0.8	−0.8	0.8
3	−2.9	−1.9	−3.5	−2.6	−1.0	−0.5	0.8
4	−4.2	−2.3			−1.0	−0.7	0.8
5		−2.6			−1.1	−1.3	0.8
6					−1.1	−2.2	0.8
7					−1.2	−3.1	0.8
8					−1.2	−3.8	0.8
13						−5.9	0.9
Unemployment (differences from base run, thousands)							
1	10	7			37	−57	84
2	50	20			76	−119	91
3	75	25			97	−178	93
4	86	23			112	−183	89
5		14			126	−169	78
6					136	−134	66
7					144	−96	57
8					149	−65	55
13						−25	50

(a) fixed interest rate
(b) fixed money target

exception of CUBS, the higher exchange rate leads to lower real output and higher levels of unemployment. All the models (except LPL, where there is an initial positive effect) produce lower inflation, this being greatest in the LBS case, where prices are $4\frac{1}{4}$ per cent lower after four years. The relatively small inflation effect in the CGP model is a result of exogenous wage determination, and this explains the greater output loss than in the NIESR and LBS models, where the larger impact on inflation stimulates the level of consumer demand.

In the CGP model lower output arises largely as a result of a decline in net exports, together with some deterioration in fixed investment, whereas in the NIESR model the effect on net exports is gradually compensated for by higher consumer and fixed investment demand.

In the LBS model the investment response is stronger than for NIESR, with the consumption effect weaker. In the NIESR model real incomes rise, whereas a fall is experienced for LBS. This reflects the real-wage effects in the two models. In the NIESR simulation prices are $2\frac{1}{2}$ per cent lower after four years with real wages unchanged, whereas prices fall by nearly the full extent of the exchange rate appreciation in the LBS simulation, with real wages $\frac{1}{2}$ per cent lower. In both models, however, the qualitative result of a return to the original level of output holds, with the speed of adjustment slightly faster in the LBS model, but with a slightly greater interim cost to output and employment.

A similar, but not identical, simulation with the HMT model under fixed interest rates (since the shock is to the residual on the exchange rate equation) gives a larger output loss than with the LBS and NIESR models, but smaller than

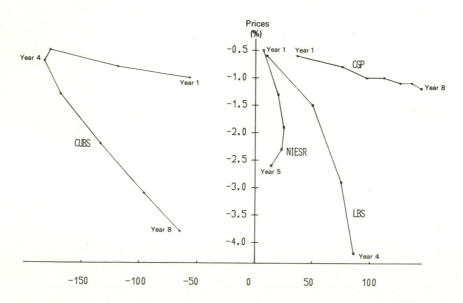

Fig. 2.6   Increase in the exchange rate: effects on unemployment and prices

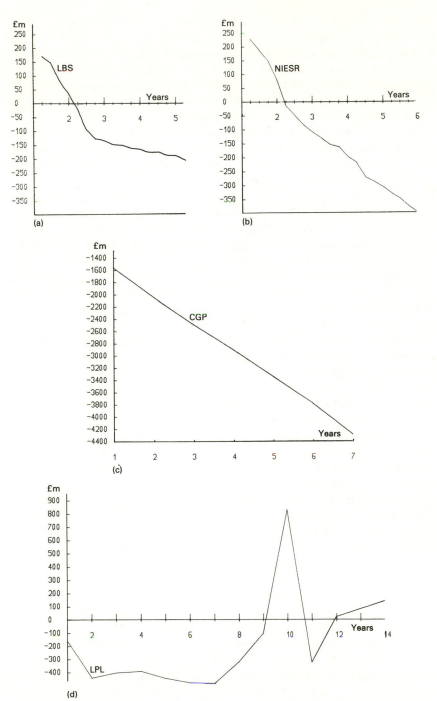

Fig. 2.7   Balance of payments effects from a 5 per cent increase in the exchange rate

that experienced in the CGP and LPL simulations, with prices some $3\frac{1}{2}$ per cent lower after four years, and with real wages virtually unchanged. In the same period the level of output is still below the original base level, but if the constant money target is used, the level of GDP is *above* the base level by the third year, with a much smaller output loss experienced in the first two years. Part of the reason for this result is that the exchange rate does not fully respond to the initial shock, only falling by $3\frac{1}{2}$ per cent after four years.

In the Liverpool model the higher real exchange rate reduces net export demand. This reduces financial wealth and lowers output expectations, thus reducing non-durable consumption. The lower level of income reduces the budget surplus, and this requires lower government spending, with the given PSBR/GDP ratio. This therefore contributes further to the fall in income. The rate of inflation in the LPL model is lower in the first year as a consequence of the reduction in real money balances relative to the fixed supply of money. There is no further impact on inflation, but real wages are reduced by around $\frac{1}{2}$ per cent (similar to the LBS result).

The CUBS model is distinct from the LPL model in that an appreciation of the real exchange rate produces a permanently higher level of output and lower level of unemployment. It also leads to lower prices ($\frac{3}{4}$ per cent after four years and $3\frac{3}{4}$ per cent after eight years). The output effect comes about in very much the same way as for the tax simulation in that a lower real wage to the employer increases labour demand and therefore output. A further contributory factor in this case is the fall in relative material prices. The dynamics of the adjustment show a negligible output effect in the third year. The output effect dies away a little over time as the decline in the real wage to employers eases. This causes a reduction in the unemployment effect despite a fall in the labour supply.

In the LPL model the 'real' current balance deteriorates at first but eventually improves marginally (see Figure 2.7). The LBS and NIESR models have the familiar J-curve effect (inverted in this case), whereby the current balance improves in the first year but subsequently worsens, as does the HMT model (Barber, 1984, p. 24). The deterioration in the current balance is greater for the NIESR than for the LBS, amounting to over £1 billion after the fourth year. In the CGP model the effect is far greater still, however, with the current balance worsening throughout, reaching £2.5 billion after the fourth year and £4.3 billion after the eighth year. (In the CUBS model the current account of the balance of payments is not distinguished.)

In the discussion of the labour market in Chapter 4, and particularly the section on wage equations (Section 4.5.3) it is argued that the long-run implications of the wage equations in the LBS, NIESR, and HMT models are that a change in the exchange rate cannot alter real wages and hence output. Full simulations with the complete models are not conclusive since they do not appear to attain a steady state within the available span of data. However, it is notable that the price level reached in the NIESR model does not respond fully to the exchange rate appreciation. This appears to be determined by the stucture of the import price relationships. The CUBS and LPL simulations are not directly comparable with the other simulations since they refer to the real exchange rate. The results of the nominal exchange rate simulations are inconclusive as to whether a higher exchange rate has a permanent effect on unemployment but they do suggest a fairly sluggish response of real wages and output.

(viii)   Increase in average earnings

In this simulation earnings are made exogenous, preventing feedback from other variables, and then are shocked by a 10 per cent increase from the values in the published forecast. In the case of CGP the shock is to total average earnings. For NIESR it is the wage rate series for the whole economy, and for LBS it is the average earnings series for manufacturing. The wage variables in the CUBS and LPL models are real wages for the whole economy. The simulation on the HMT model shown is not strictly comparable since the equation residual is shocked, leading to a change in earnings of 13 per cent in year 1 and 32 per cent by year 4 for the fixed interest rate case (13 and 21 per cent , respectively, in the fixed money target case).

All the models show (Table 2.8) that an increase in earnings reduces the level of output and increases price inflation, but there are some very contrasting results. In the NIESR model output increases initially as higher earnings increase real wages sharply and hence total real incomes and consumption. After five years real wages are still 2 per cent higher, but by now price adjustment has taken place and the exchange rate has fallen by nearly 9 per cent. Then lower consumption and investment activity offset the improvement in net exports, but the decline in output is much less severe than in the other models.

Output effects in the CGP, CUBS, and LBS models are fairly similar, the main difference between CGP and CUBS being that the peak decline in output of $1\frac{3}{4}$ per cent is maintained for CGP, whereas the CUBS effect peaks at 3 per cent and then declines steadily.

The changes to output in the CGP model come about from a rise in consumption which is moderated over time as the price effects work through, coupled with falling exports and fixed investment where the effect builds up over time. Here real wages rise by over 3 per cent more than in the NIESR simulation and more than in the LBS case, where the rise is 1 per cent. In the CUBS model the *real* wage shock of 10 per cent operates through the labour market rather than through incomes, so that employment demand is reduced and labour supply increased. The reduction in employment demand reduces output through the production function. Once labour demand and supply have adjusted to the new real wage there are no further effects from this source, but the assumption of endogenous money determination introduces a cumulative effect on inflation which maintains output some $\frac{1}{4}$ per cent below its original level.

For the LBS the price adjustment operates quite quickly and the exchange rate falls by 4 per cent as the domestic money stock rises. The initial impact on

Table 2.8   *Earnings simulation*

10% increase in earnings

Year	LBS	NIESR	HMT (a)	HMT (b)	CGP	CUBS	LPL
GDP (% differences from base run)							
1	−0.4	0.9	1.0	−0.4	−0.5	−0.5	−3.1
2	−1.8	0.2	−0.8	−3.2	−1.3	−1.9	−2.9
3	−1.9	−0.6	−2.2	−4.4	−1.6	−3.0	−2.9
4	−1.7	−0.7	−2.8	−4.6	−1.6	−2.0	−2.8
5		−0.7			−1.7	−1.6	−2.8
6					−1.7	−1.1	−3.0
7					−1.8	−0.6	−3.2
8					−1.8	−0.4	−3.5
13						−0.3	−4.6
Prices (% differences from base run)							
1	3.7	2.5	5.0	4.8	3.8	0.1	0.8
2	8.4	6.0	11.4	8.8	5.5	0.5	1.0
3	9.0	7.0	16.4	10.6	6.2	1.2	1.0
4	9.0	7.5	19.6	11.0	6.6	3.5	1.0
5		7.8			6.7	6.9	1.2
6					6.8	10.7	1.5
7					6.8	14.0	1.6
8					6.8	16.4	1.4
13						21.5	5.8
Unemployment (differences from base run, thousands)							
1	−27	−74			45	470	919
2	−133	−65			113	910	1354
3	−76	5			168	1060	1449
4	40	57			206	948	1383
5		89			233	738	1234
6					254	503	1088
7					271	338	971
8					286	264	896
13						186	707

(*a*) fixed interest rate
(*b*) fixed money target

consumption is favourable while the transitional real wage effects exist, but as these are eroded, and as the level of price inflation itself lowers consumer spending (together with lower investment from higher money stock), the output effect builds up.

The LPL model shows the greatest short- and long-run impact on output (but the smallest on inflation). Higher real wages increase the equilibrium level of unemployment and lower equilibrium output, raising the equilibrium exchange rate. The rise in interest rates causes a reduction of financial wealth leading to a fall in spending in goods and services. The small increase in inflation in this model is due to the fixed stock of money (given by the PSBR/GDP ratio) relative to a decline in real money balances as a result of higher interest rates and lower private wealth.

The size of the unemployment repercussions in the model is striking. Equilibrium unemployment increases by nearly 1 million in the LPL model. In the CUBS model it peaks at around this level after two or three years, before falling to $\frac{1}{4}$ million, a level also reached by CGP. In comparison, the unemployment effects in the LBS and NIESR models are quite small. Unemployment *falls* in both cases during the first two years and continues to fall in the third year for LBS. This effect is explained by the initial increase in output in the NIESR model, whereas in the LBS model the unemployment effect is largely due to a rise in employment in the primary and tertiary sectors, where the effect on consumption operating through retail sales is quite strong.

The balance of payments on current account deteriorates by £2.5 billion in the first year of the CGP simulation with the scale of deterioration rising to reach £8.5 billion after eight years. However, in the LBS and NIESR models the fall in the exchange rate that accompanies the rise in earnings turns the initial fall in the current balance into a surplus by the fourth year of the simulation, with the improvement more marked in the NIESR case than for LBS (£4 billion as against £0.3 billion).

All the models appear to be quite sensitive to these two key variables, the exchange rate and wages. Price inflation effects are quite large in both cases with some sizeable output and unemployment effects in the earnings simulation. Given past failures in modelling the exchange rate and earnings variables, these simulations give some measure of the sensitivity of forecasts and simulations to these particular structures.

The discussion so far has been concerned very much with the development of unemployment, output and inflation under the various simulations. In the next section we look at some particularly relevant ratios implicit in the results.

2.4 Comparative public sector costs

Another means of comparing model simulations is to examine their 'cost' in terms of the increase/decrease in the fiscal deficit necessary to create additional employment. In respect of fiscal policies, the ratio of the change in the PSBR to the change in employment resulting from implementation of the policy provides a guide to its comparative efficiency in boosting labour demand. Those models in which multipliers are high and labour demand depends primarily on output rather than on relative prices generally suggest that the fiscal costs of expanding labour demand are relatively low. On the other hand, in those models where output is determined primarily from the supply side, one would expect the PSBR/employment ratio to be high, particularly in the longer run. In some cases the ratio changes sign over time: in this circumstance it has to be interpreted with care. In some cases it is permanently negative as, for example, where an increase in world trade simultaneously boosts labour demand and cuts the PSBR. Similarly, fiscal shocks with some of the models may simultaneously crowd out private spending and increase the relative price of labour. The resultant fall in employment and increase in the PSBR will also yield negative values for the ratio.

This ratio provides a useful summary measure, and for each policy simulation we plot its trajectory over time. Note however that, since employment is a stock and the PBSR is a flow, the value of the ratio gives the expected *recurrent* fiscal cost of each additional job created by the shock. Alternatively, since the economy cannot escape a process of adjustment following a disturbance, one might use the expected *accrued* fiscal cost as the appropriate measure. In most cases both ratios will convey the same information, though when sign changes occur, both should be considered. Note further that the PSBR is expressed in nominal terms and is not discounted. Hence one should interpret the results conditional on current and past inflation rates and interest rates, which have been discussed earlier in this chapter.

First consider the results from the LBS model. The trajectories of the four fiscal shocks, namely increased government spending, reduced income tax, increased VAT and reduced state benefits, are shown in Figure 2.8, and a brief comparative study is given in Table 2.9. Two implications concerning the behaviour of the LBS model are immediately obvious from the figure. First, the model does not stabilize quickly in response to the changed level of the fiscal instrument. In none of the experiments do *both* the change in the PSBR and the change in employment return to rough constancy by the end of the period. This finding is relevant to the discussion of steady states and dynamics below. Second, it is apparent that the model implies that there are substantial differences in the 'efficiency' of the different policies. These range from the apparent success of increasing VAT, which both cuts the PSBR and raises the

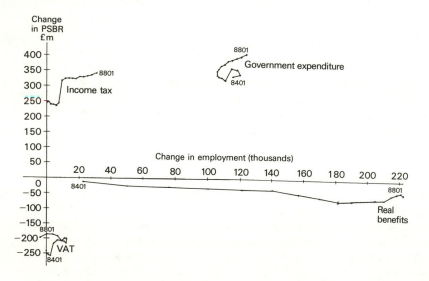

Fig. 2.8   PSBR-employment trajectories: LBS model

Table 2.9   *PSBR/employment ratio in the fiscal shock simulations*
(Figures relate to year 4 of each simulation)

Model	LBS	NIESR	CGP	CUBS	LPL
		(£ *thousand*)			
Government expenditure	13.5	−2.8	9.8	10.8	23.7[a] 18.8[b]
Income tax	55.1	5.2	49.2	−1.2	−2.6
VAT rate	−144.1	44.5	36.5	−2.3	−
Unemployment benefit	−0.8	−	−	−10.4	0.7

[a] Accommodating PSBR/GDP ratio
[b] Non-accommodating PSBR/GDP ratio

level of employment (albeit temporarily), to extremely costly income tax cuts, where a heavy fiscal cost is paid for a fairly small increase in employment.

On a more detailed examination of the results it is apparent that much of the explanation of their differences lies with changes in productivity. In both the VAT and real benefit simulations, output falls yet employment rises. When government spending is increased or income tax reduced, output increases along with employment. The key to these findings lies partly in the ability of price signals to offset the quantity effects in determining the demand for labour. For example, the volume of real unemployment benefits enters the equation for employment in the primary, residual and tertiary sectors and, moreover, forms part of its long-run solution. Hence, cuts in benefits directly expand the demand for labour in this sector. Increasing VAT has a detrimental effect on output but real wage costs are brought down. The net effect on unemployment is negligible, as is the net effect in the income tax simulation. Thus, an *increase* in indirect taxes of around £800 million per year differs little in its effect on the labour market from a *decrease* in direct taxes amounting to approximately £1.1 billion. The unemployment benefit and government spending simulations, by contrast, imply increases in total employment of approximately 0.5 and 1 per cent, respectively. However, the government spending experiment must be treated with caution. In order to effect the required increase in spending, an exogenous increase of 100,000 in public sector employment has been made. In fact, the increase in private sector employment resulting from the shock is very small, averaging around 15,000.

Thus these experiments with the LBS model suggest that standard fiscal measures which do not directly impinge on the labour market will have little impact on the demand and supply of labour in the private sector. The current version of the LBS model is thus unlikely to respond favourably to interventionist measures in the traditional Keynesian sense. However, it does not extract

too high an inflationary cost for interventions of the magnitude already discussed. Indeed, the increase in government expenditure actually results in a
lower rate of price inflation owing to a stronger currency appreciation in the
early part of the simulation period than is evident from the other experiments.

The inflationary response of the NIESR model to the various fiscal stimuli is
similarly muted, though the government expenditure shock does cause a rise of
2.2 per cent in the level of the price index in year 5, contrasting sharply with the
LBS results. The greater contrast between the two models, however, lies in the
differences in the PSBR/employment ratio under the various shocks (Figure 2.9).
Comparison of the government expenditure shock is again complicated by the
exogenous increase of 100,000 in government employment in the LBS model.
Each additional job created as a result of a 5 per cent reduction in income tax
rates costs £13,500 four years into the LBS simulation, while the corresponding
figure for the NIESR model is £2800. While initially the impact on the PSBR of
the tax reduction is approximately equal in both models, their behaviour during
the simulation is consistently divergent, with a continuing increase in the LBS
model contrasting with a pronounced fall in the PSBR in the NIESR model.
Part of the explanation of this difference clearly lies in the labour market itself:
the impact of the tax change on the labour market is felt much more rapidly in
the NIESR model. With unemployment falling and employment rising, tax payments are increased, thus offsetting the initial increase in the fiscal deficit.
Another factor contributing to the smaller PSBR effects in the NIESR model is
the constancy of the cost of public expenditure between the base run and the
expenditure simulation. In contrast, the LBS model adjusts the cost of expenditure for the effects of high inflation.

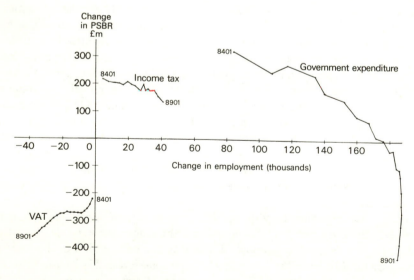

Fig. 2.9   PSBR–employment trajectories: NIESR model

A simulation of the NIESR model yielding an equivalent increase in the tax rate on consumer expenditure to a 10 per cent increase in the VAT rate also diverges widely from the LBS results. In contrast to LBS, both the PSBR *and* employment fall, implying an average saving of £44,500 on the PSBR in the fourth year of the simulation for each job lost. The NIESR model lacks the more intricate productivity effects contained in the LBS model. Employment hence is linked more directly to the expenditure aggregates whose size and composition fluctuate in response to fiscal shocks. In consequence, reduced demand in the goods market is transmitted directly to a similar effect on the labour market.

The simulated increase of £200 million in government sector spending directly increases employment in public administration and defence by 56,000. It also increases equilibrium employment in 'mainly public industries' by approximately 1.8 per cent or around 40,000. Thus, the NIESR results, which imply that the ratio of the PSBR to employment runs negative in the fourth year of the simulation, are heavily weighted towards employment creation in the public sector.

Like the NIESR model, the CGP model does not include unemployment benefits as a policy instrument and hence can simulate benefit reductions only through their effects on aggregate demand rather than supply. The models are also similar in the direction of their response to the income tax, VAT and government spending simulations. With the change in the PSBR and the change in employment having the same sign in each simulation, the impression is again of the adjustment of the labour market to the goods market being based primarily on quantity rather than price adjustment. There are wide differences again in the relative effectiveness of the different policies with the reduction in income tax, at £49,000 per job in the fourth year of the simulation, being the most costly because of a rapid leakage of demand through imports. The VAT increase reduces the PSBR by £36,500 for every job lost, while increased government spending apparently increases employment at a cost of only £9800 per job in the fourth year of the simulation. As in the LBS and NIESR government expenditure experiments, the resulting increase in employment is largely concentrated in the public sector.

Apart from the differences in magnitude, the other most distinctive feature of the CGP responses is their apparent stability. Variables tend to increase or decrease monotonically at a fairly constant rate. By contrast, the quarterly models exhibit more cyclical response patterns. The CGP model has been developed with medium- to long-term forecasting in mind and thus places less emphasis on the stock cycle, which has played a major role in recent UK economic cycles. However, it is apparent from the simulations of the quarterly models that shocks to fiscal variables do not, in general, trigger violent swings in stockholding. Rather, the cyclical response in the quarterly models has more to do with the internal dynamics of other behavioural equations than with the behaviour of stocks.

With annual models such as CUBS and LPL, a qualitatively different response to the fiscal simulations might be expected. Some of the results are, however, surprisingly consonant with those from the other models. For example, in the CUBS model an increase in government spending boosts the PSBR by £1.8 billion four years into the simulation and at the same time increases employment by 163,000 (see Figure 2.10). These results are similar to those derived from the

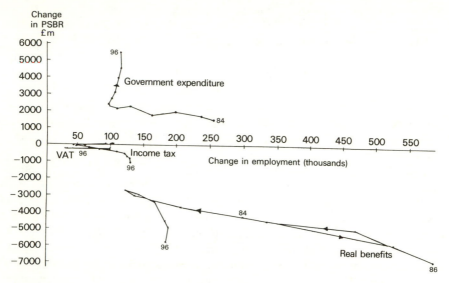

Fig. 2.10   PSBR–employment trajectories: CUBS model

LBS model four years into the simulations. A difference in composition is evident, however. Private sector employment is crowded out by the expansion of public spending (as a result of greater sensitivity to real wages). Thus, while the net employment effect is positive in both models, private sector employment falls by 65,000 in the CUBS simulation but rises by 16,000 with the LBS model. In the Liverpool model with an accommodating PSBR, employment rises quite sharply initially, but after two years begins to fall back so that by the end of the simulation it is virtually unaffected (see Figure 2.11). With a non-accommodating PSBR, inflation does not rise so rapidly and private sector spending is more robust. Employment does not rise so rapidly in the first two years, but by the end of the simulations it has increased to a slightly higher level than under the accommodating PSBR scenario.

The output response of the CUBS and LPL models to an income tax shock never exceeds 1 per cent throughout their respective simulations. Neither are real wages dramatically affected by the change in disposable income. The net result on the labour market is consequently fairly modest. In the LPL model there is a substantial rise in private sector spending, but the fixed PSBR/GDP ratio implies concomitant cutbacks in public sector expenditure so that, while the distribution of employment between the private and public sectors changes

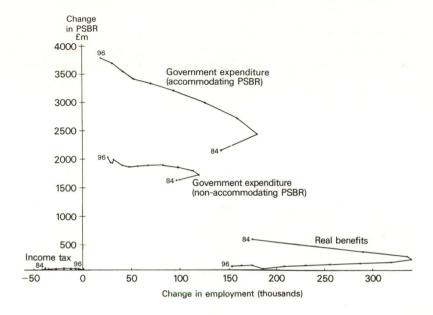

Fig. 2.11   PSBR–employment trajectories: LPL model

during the simulation, there is only a negligible impact on total employment by the end of the period.

Direct labour market intervention elicits much more dramatic effects from both models. Following a 10 per cent cut in real unemployment benefits, private sector employment increases by 7 per cent after four years in the CUBS simulation before gradually declining to a level 1.7 per cent higher in year 13. Employment in utilities increases by a small amount and then declines, while government employment is unaffected. The improvement in the labour market is accompanied by a decline in the PSBR as a proportion of GDP.

In the LPL model, a fall in the equilibrium real wage resulting from the cut in benefits causes an expansion of employment by a maximum of 341,000 in year 4. Output increases slightly and, because the PSBR/GDP ratio is fixed, the PSBR actually increases. This characteristic places the PSBR/employment trajectory in the first quadrant of Figure 2.11, whereas it might be more in keeping with the philosophy of the LPL model that it be in the second quadrant (employment rising/PSBR falling).

2.5   Dynamic aspects of the model comparisons

As with many previous exercises, the simulations studied in this chapter were chosen on primarily economic grounds, considering their plausibility and interest, given the past behaviour of the economy. In this section we comment briefly on the evidence they present on the dynamic behaviour of the models.

An important question is whether a particular model returns to a 'steady state' following an exogenous shock. If one could, perhaps crudely, divide the simulation period into parts where short-run and long-run impacts predominate respectively, then one could more readily interpret a given set of simulation results in the light of the predictions of economic theory. It is clear, however, from the preceding discussion that different models appear to settle down at different rates following an exogenous shock, this finding being the result of differences in dynamic structure and in the level of temporal aggregation of the models. Further, given that some of the forecast databases available for the models are quite short, the simulation results occasionally suggest that a model might have become unstable had additional exogenous data similar in characteristics to the existing dataset been available.

The problem of identifying 'steady states' can be linked to the study of the 'great ratios' as identified by Klein (1979), who argues that the credibility of models is partly dependent on their ability to maintain rough constancy in variables such as the wage share, savings rate, and velocity of money. During the last decade, such variables have moved quite widely in response to external shocks, but have shown a tendency to return to trend values, if not constancy, when the stimulus is removed. Figure 2.12 shows how the wage share, savings ratio and velocity of money behave in the LBS model when some of the standard simulations are carried out. What is most noticeable is the narrow range of variation of the ratios, showing how little they are affected by the different simulations. Clearly, two variables might individually exhibit considerable instability while their ratio remains constant. Thus, the stability of these ratios, albeit noteworthy, does not imply that the model as a whole behaves in a stable fashion.

The sluggish behaviour exhibited by the ratios under the different simulations suggests that numerator and denominator are perhaps too closely coupled to permit the type of fluctuation that is consistent with recent experience. Alternatively, one might take the view that the restricted set of impulses contained in the simulations are insufficient to excite the various models into more plausible modes of response. One finding that is apparent from the simulations is that there is more variation in these ratios in both the historical data and in the base (forecast) run of the model than in the model simulations. Since the experiments were designed to elicit the economic properties of the models, by providing matrices of partial derivatives of endogenous variables with respect to exogenous variables for comparison with prior notions derived from economic theory, it is not surprising that they say relatively little about overall dynamic properties. To obtain further information on model dynamics requires experiments designed for the purpose, using a wider range of input signals with known properties in the time and frequency domains. Other techniques that might allow a direct examination of the long-run properties of the model in the nonlinear case are under investigation.

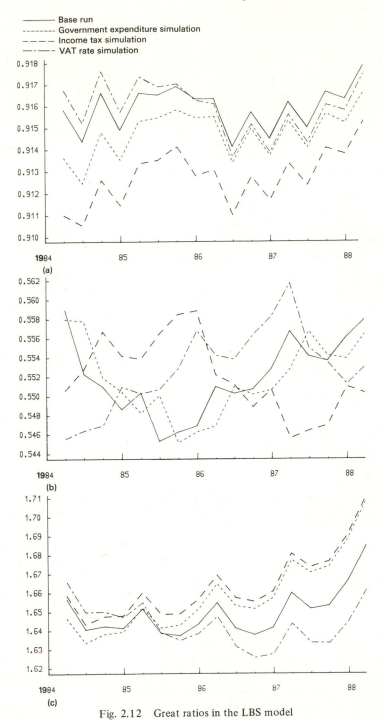

Fig. 2.12   Great ratios in the LBS model

2.6   Summary and conclusions

In this chapter we have compared six macroeconomic models under a variety of shocks. These simulations provide a summary of the model responses under the various exogeneity assumptions and residual adjustments incorporated in the base run (in most cases, the respective published forecasts). The results can be used as ready-reckoners to calculate the impact of shocks of alternative magnitude subject to a nonlinearity caveat and the proviso that the alternative shocks do not drive the model outside the range of experience over which it provides a good approximation. While a modeller might use simulation results to assess the adequacy of the model, perhaps revising the structure if results that are in some way implausible are observed, our objectives of description and comparison have been more modest.

The results for the government expenditure simulation show a considerable divergence in the relative unemployment–inflation trade-offs and in the extent to which the private sector is crowded out (or in). The most favourable trade-offs appear in the CGP, LBS, and NIESR models (there is some crowding in the latter two cases), and the worst trade-offs are in the LPL and CUBS models. However, these results depend crucially on the financing assumption (as illustrated by the HMT simulations), which vary considerably between the models. The results of the government expenditure simulations are also dependent on the way the models handle the implied increases in public sector employment. For a reduction in income tax rates LPL is the only model not to show an increase in output in the short run. For CGP and NIESR (and LBS in the short run), the relative GDP effects from the public expenditure and tax simulations suggest a balanced budget multiplier of greater than zero but less than one. However, in terms of the inflation–unemployment trade-off LBS is the only model to reveal unequivocally a preference for government expenditure increases over tax cuts. The variation in the unemployment effects between the models is greater in the tax rate simulation than for the government expenditure simulation with the inflation effects differing in direction between the models.

As far as external shocks are concerned, the effect of higher world demand is seen to be beneficial for output in all the models. Conventional wisdom used to regard the effects of an increase in oil prices as similar to that from an increase in VAT. However, the presence of domestic oil production has complicated the issue and this is reflected in the models. Output effects are now seen to be quite small, and some of the models (i.e. LBS and NIESR) possess the property that domestic inflation falls. This effect arises from the impact of oil prices on the value of domestic oil reserves and hence on the exchange rate.

All the models appear to be quite sensitive to the earnings and exchange rate variables. The results of the nominal exchange rate simulations are inconclusive as to whether a higher exchange rate has a permanent effect on unemployment, but they do suggest a very sluggish response of real wages and output.

An examination of the public finance costs of alternative fiscal policies expressed in terms of the employment generated reveals not only a marked divergence between the cost of different methods of generating the same employment effect, but also major differences between the effects using the same policy instrument in the different models.

Turning to more general issues, the differences between the patterns of responses in the annual and quarterly models tend to be smaller than perhaps might have been expected. CUBS is the only model to generate any notable cycle in its response, and this reflects the change in financing assumption in 1986 rather than model structure. Thus, the role of stockbuilding emerges as a rather passive one which is smooth in contrast to the marked variations observed in the historical data. Similar observations can be made from examination of the 'great ratios' where there appear to be negligible changes in the simulation values relative to major variations in the historical data. These results may, of course, merely reflect the inappropriateness of the input shock.

It is very difficult to describe the long-run properties of the models from these simulations. In many cases the model may not have converged to a steady state by the end of the simulation period, and in several cases there is a suggestion that the model may be 'exploding'. Simply extending the time horizon of the simulations is not necessarily a solution to this problem, since the underlying base run required for this purpose may take the model far outside its accustomed range of variation. In addition, whether the long run has been reached rests on a subjective judgement. The issues of appropriate input shocks and methods of examining the long-run nature of macroeconomic models remain open research problems.

Chapter 3

Forecast Comparisons

3.1 Introduction

Comparative tabulations of macroeconomic forecasts often appear in the press and are undoubtedly of interest, but they provide no explanation of perceived differences among forecasts. This chapter analyses the variation between forecasts. We take four forecasts from different groups all made at approximately the same time, ensuring that differences in the information sets available to the forecasters are minimized as far as possible. We then explain differences between the forecasts in terms of different assumptions regarding exogenous inputs, the influence of judgement on the forecasts and differences between the underlying economic models. The analysis is based on the set of models and input and adjustment files supplied to the Bureau by the model proprietors. The models were solved using Bureau software guaranteeing a consistent treatment. The term 'forecast' is interpreted generically to include conditional projections of the economy which some model teams may wish to distinguish from forecasts of future outcomes.

The four forecasts comprise two quarterly forecasts (LBS and NIESR) and two annual forecasts (CUBS and LPL). In the general description we also include the forecast based on the Cambridge Growth Project model, but as it is prepared privately by Cambridge Econometrics Ltd (CE) it is not included in the more formal analysis in Sections 3.4 and 3.5. As noted in Chapter 1, these forecasts were generally made in the autumn of 1983, with the CE forecast slightly earlier (July 1983) and the Liverpool forecast slightly later. The re-basing of the National Accounts to a 1980-price database took place in autumn 1983, and, to the extent that it introduced a different view of the recent past, it might be expected to influence those forecasts computed after the re-basing exercise. In fact, only the CE forecast was made prior to rebasing. The apparent differences in the price base of the published forecasts of NIESR and LBS are due to the re-scaling of the 1975-price-based forecast to 1980 prices in the NIESR publication. This re-scaling results in some minor differences from the 1975-price-based forecast which is discussed here.

Differences in data frequency and time horizons pose problems of comparison. In general, one might expect quarterly models to be more appropriate for diagnosing and predicting economic turning points, whereas the annual models might be thought to be more appropriate for revealing medium-term trends in the economy. In fact, the LBS forecast extends to 1988, not far short of the horizon of the Cambridge forecast (1990). The NIESR also published a medium-term forecast to 1989 at the same time as their short-term forecast (to the beginning of 1986), but this forecast is not on a consistent basis with the short-term forecast so we restrict attention to the latter. The CUBS and LPL forecasts extend considerably further than the others (1996 and 1997, respectively). One major difference in the nature of the forecasts is where terminal conditions of certain variables, particularly inflation, are set in the LPL model. No such features exist in the other models.

In his study Artis (1982) sets out a four-fold classification of the differences between forecasts. First, there may be differences in the information set available on the recent past; second, there may be differences in the judgement exercised to produce the forecast path of equation residuals or constant adjustments; third, there may be variations in the paths set for exogenous variables; and finally, the models themselves differ both in their economic structure and in the set of variables considered to be exogenous.

We are unable to analyse the effects of different information sets without knowing how the teams would have acted with different information. These differences are likely to have been small for the three forecasts (CUBS, LBS, and NIESR) made within a few weeks of each other, whereas CE would have had a more dated, and Liverpool a more recent, set of information. Some of the timing differences, however, may have led to different projections of exogenous variables, and this effect is captured by standardizing the exogenous assumption used in the models.

Where more than one projection of the economy is given, as in the CUBS forecast, we select the central view. All of the forecasts/projections assume a fiscal and monetary policy stance consistent with the Medium-Term Financial Strategy (MTFS) of the government. However the MTFS does not indicate an exact set of policy instrument changes. While indexing allowances, NIESR does not make any fiscal adjustments for adherence to the MTFS, whereas all other groups make adjustments to specific policy instruments based on their best guesses as to policy decisions that are consistent with the MTFS. They allow for some reduction in tax rates, but the timing and magnitude of these changes varies between the forecasts. This and other problems involved in modelling monetary and fiscal policy stance are taken up in Chapter 5.

Section 3.2 gives a summary of the key economic indicators from the various forecasts with a brief discussion of the differences between them. In Section 3.3 the comparative exogenous assumptions are described and the models are then re-run on a set of common assumptions in order to analyse the differences in the forecasts arising from exogenous assumptions. Section 3.4 outlines the type of residual adjustments made to the models and derives alternative forecasts based on rules that attempt to extract the role of judgement in the forecasts. In Section 3.5 we decompose the forecasts, following the example of Artis (1982), into differences arising from exogenous assumptions, differences arising from residual judgements and differences arising from the models themselves. The final section provides a summary and conclusions.

3.2   Summary of the forecasts

Much of the interest surrounding economic forecasts tends to be in their implications for inflation and unemployment. The various forecasts are shown in
inflation–unemployment space in Figure 3.1. The 1983 figures differ because
they themselves are 'forecasts', based on perhaps as little as six months' information for that year.

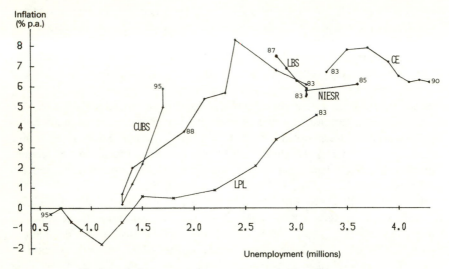

Fig. 3.1   Inflation–unemployment relationships in the forecasts

The Liverpool forecast is the most optimistic, with inflation becoming
negative and unemployment declining from 3 million in 1983 to just over
$\frac{1}{2}$ million by 1995. The CUBS forecast also implies a combination of falling
inflation and unemployment after 1985 until 1991, but this follows a period of
rising inflation coupled with a decline in unemployment in 1984 and 1985 and is
in turn followed by rising inflation and slightly rising unemployment after 1991.
LBS forecasts a steady rise in inflation combined with falling unemployment,
whereas CE predict falling inflation and an increase in unemployment. Only the
NIESR forecast reveals a deterioration in both inflation and unemployment. In
terms of Figure 3.1, clearly, the more pessimistic forecasts, such as CE, tend to
be in the north-east quadrant, while the more optimistic lie in the south-west
quadrant.

Other summary indicators of the forecasts are shown in Table 3.1. Estimates
of growth for 1983 vary considerably. NIESR and CUBS use the output measure
of GDP, which produces a lower growth rate for 1983 than does the expenditure
measure used by LBS. LPL also use the expenditure measure, but with more
recent information this model has a higher estimate of GDP for 1983.

Over the short term (to 1985), the CUBS forecast predicts the most rapid
recovery of output. In fact, CUBS are the only team expecting an acceleration in

Table 3.1   *Forecasts compared*

	1983	1984	1985	1986	1987-90	1991-95	Cumulative growth 1983-85
GDP (growth % p.a.)							
LBS	2.5	1.9	2.4	1.7	1.1*	..	4.3
NIESR	2.2	2.0	1.0	..	..	..	4.1
CE	2.5	2.5	1.6	1.5	1.3	..	4.1
CUBS	2.2	4.9	3.3	0.2	2.1	1.9	8.4
LPL	3.6	3.5	3.0	4.3	4.7	4.0	6.6
Average	2.6	3.0	2.3	1.9	2.3	3.0	5.3
Inflation (% p.a.)							
LBS	5.6	5.9	6.3	6.9	7.5*	..	12.5
NIESR	5.5	5.8	6.1	..	..	..	12.2
CE	6.7	8.0	7.9	7.2	6.3	..	16.5
CUBS	6.1	6.8	8.3	5.7	3.7	2.9	15.7
LPL	4.6	3.4	2.1	0.9	−0.4	−0.8	5.6
Average	5.7	6.0	6.1	5.2	4.3	1.1	12.5
Unemployment (millions)							
LBS	3.1	3.1	3.0	2.9	2.8*	..	..
NIESR	3.1	3.3	3.6	..	..	..	..
CE	3.3	3.5	3.7	3.9	4.1	..	..
CUBS	3.1	2.8	2.4	2.3	1.6	1.9	..
LPL	3.0	2.8	2.6	2.2	1.4	0.8	..
Average	3.1	3.1	3.1	2.8	2.5	1.4	..
PSBR (£ billion)							
LBS	10.9	8.3	6.7	5.2	4.7*	..	
NIESR	7.8	9.8	10.2	..	..	..	
CE	10.2	11.7	13.3	16.0	19.8	..	
CUBS	7.3	1.1	−5.6	−3.6	1.8	3.3	
LPL	9.5	6.8	5.4	4.1	2.8	1.7	
Average	9.1	7.5	6.0	5.4	7.3	2.5	
Money supply (% p.a.)							
LBS (£M₃)	11.9	10.5	9.4	9.1	9.2*	..	
NIESR (£M₃)	11.3	11.2	11.2	..	..	..	
CE (£M₃)	11.6	12.2	12.5	12.1	10.7	..	
CUBS (M0)	9.0	8.2	7.3	6.3	2.7	3.5	
LPL (M₁)	5.6	12.1	9.8	9.1	7.2	2.0	

* 1987 only

the growth rate in 1984, the other groups forecasting either a steady rate of recovery (CE, LPL, NIESR) or a moderate easing in the rate of growth of output (LBS). The range of forecasts of output growth is 3 per cent in 1984, and $2\frac{1}{4}$ per cent in 1985, the same as the average forecast growth in these years. The degree of variability in the forecasts is therefore substantial. All, except LBS, foresee a slackening in the growth rate in 1985. The short-term recovery is sufficient to result in a fall in the level of unemployment only in the cases of CUBS and LPL, while CE and NIESR predict a steady rise in unemployment. LPL are the only group to see a continuation of the reduction in inflation over the period to 1985.

As with the output forecasts, the range of the forecasts of inflation is large, being $4\frac{1}{2}$ per cent in 1984 and $6\frac{1}{4}$ per cent in 1985 with a mean forecast of 6 per cent in both years.

There are problems in comparing the medium-term forecasts because the various forecasts all have different horizons. While the CUBS forecast is the most optimistic in terms of growth in the short-term, it is considerably more pessi-mistic than Liverpool over the following decade. In the CUBS forecast growth comes abruptly to a halt in 1986 and 1987 before resuming in 1988, averaging just under 2 per cent per annum over the rest of the forecast period. In contrast, growth in the LPL forecast is quite rapid and unprecedented by historical standards, averaging over 4 per cent per annum between 1985 and 1997. The LBS and CE forecasts fall at the more pessimistic end of the range, both fore-casting average growth of under $1\frac{1}{2}$ per cent per annum (1985–7 for LBS and 1985–90 for CE). The range of medium-term forecasts of output growth is there-fore no less substantial than that of the short-term forecasts.

The differences in the medium-term outlook for inflation and unemployment are also striking. LPL actually predicts a whole decade of falling prices, whereas CE and LBS predict inflation averaging 6–7 per cent per annum over their respective horizons. The CUBS forecast lies between the two sets with inflation remaining around 6 per cent in 1986 before easing to just over 3 per cent per annum between 1987 and 1995. A similar pattern holds for forecasts of unem-ployment, with the CUBS forecast holding the middle ground between the optimistic LPL forecast ($\frac{1}{2}$ million by 1997) and the more pessimistic LBS and CE forecasts.

The contributions of items of expenditure to GDP growth over the periods 1983–5 and 1985–7 are shown in Table 3.2. The CUBS model is not built around an expenditure framework and hence does not permit such a decompo-sition. Table 3.2 represents an accounting framework for describing differences between expenditure components of the forecasts and cannot be interpreted causally, so it should not be inferred that the aggregates in any sense lead to the output growth reported.

Of the four forecasts for 1983–5, LPL has the most buoyant growth. This is due largely to domestic final demand, although there is a contribution from the net trade balance. Both private non-durable consumption and private durable expenditure (consumer durables, fixed investment, and stockbuilding) contrib-ute equally to the expansion of demand. The contribution of non-durable con-sumption is similar in the LBS forecast. Here the main role of the remainder of private demand is far weaker, although public expenditure is more expansionary than for the Liverpool forecast. Changes in the trade balance have a negligible impact, as they do in the more pessimistic NIESR forecast. Almost all of the difference between the NIESR and LBS growth forecasts is attributable to the differences in private consumption. For the period 1983–5 the CE forecast lies

Table 3.2 *Expenditure contributions to output growth**

	1983–85				1985–87		
	LBS	NIESR	CE	LPL	LBS	CE	LPL
Private non-durable consumption	2.67 ⎫	0.61	2.42	3.13	2.29 ⎫	2.94	4.35
Private durable consumption	0.16 ⎭				–		
Stockbuilding	0.41	0.89	0.40	3.29 ⎫	–	–	4.72 ⎫
Private investment	1.08	0.78	1.52		0.19	0.70	
Public investment	0.50	0.13	0.17	–	0.34	0.17	–
Public consumption	0.23	0.64	0.18		0.37	0.38	
Domestic final demand	5.05	3.05	4.69	6.42	3.19	4.19	9.07
Trade balance**	0.06	0.32	–	1.18	–	–0.74	0.71
Residual between output/exp.GDP	0.48 ⎫	–0.34	–0.64	..	–	–0.80	–
Factor cost adjustment	–0.65 ⎭			–1.94	–0.46		–1.32
GDP growth (per cent.)	4.94	3.03	4.05	6.60	2.78	2.65	8.50

* Figures do not add up exactly owing to rounding.
** Exports less imports.

somewhere between the NIESR and LBS forecasts of demand, with the contribution of private investment quite strong.

Over the period 1985–7 the differences between the LBS and LPL forecasts are more striking than in the earlier period. All components of demand are more buoyant in the LPL forecast, but of particular note is the strong growth of private expenditure (other than on non-durable consumption). This rapid growth in the LPL forecast arises from the impact of a falling inflation rate on the stock of real financial wealth held by the private sector. Lower inflation increases real wealth, and portfolio balance considerations lead to an adjustment to the desired stock of goods which results in an increase in expenditure on real assets. The CE forecast of demand is more buoyant than that of LBS, but this is offset by a deterioration in the trade balance.

In the CE, LBS, and NIESR forecasts the rate of productivity growth eases as GDP growth slows down, but this is most marked in the case of LBS, where productivity growth almost comes to a halt in 1986–7. The rate of productivity growth in the CUBS and LPL models bears no simple relationship to output growth. In the CUBS forecast productivity actually falls by 4 per cent between 1985 and 1988 before picking up to an average of 1-$1\frac{1}{2}$ per cent per annum for the remainder of the forecast. The implied rate of growth in the LPL forecast is the most rapid of all the forecasts.

The development of real wages and employment is shown in Figure 3.2. Estimates of the base year position again differ, not only because the 1983 figure is an estimate but also because of definitional matters affecting employment. Expansion of employment is coupled with a falling real wage in the CE and CUBS forecasts (to 1987), while the LPL and CUBS forecasts (the latter after 1987) show a positive association between real wages and employment.

There is a marked difference in the financial aspects of the forecasts, shown in Figure 3.3. The base year positions are now further apart owing to differences in

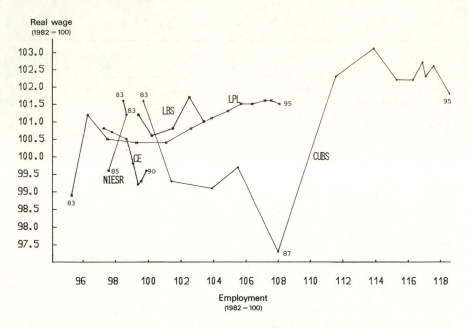

Fig. 3.2   Real wage–employment relationships in the forecasts

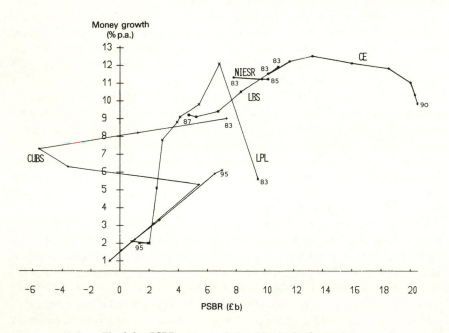

Fig. 3.3   PSBR–money relationships in the forecasts

the money stock concept employed; nevertheless, comparison of the trajectories remains of interest. CE and NIESR predict either a steady or accelerating rate of increase in the money stock coupled with a rising PSBR between 1983 and 1985, whereas LBS forecasts a steady decline in both. After 1985 the PSBR continues to rise in the CE forecast but this is reflected in a gradual decline in the rate of monetary expansion, while the latter stays steady in the LBS forecast despite a fall in the PSBR. After a brief surge in monetary growth to 12 per cent in 1984, the LPL forecast suggests a steady decline in both the PSBR and the growth of money, bottoming out at around £2 billion and 2 per cent respectively in the mid nineties. The PSBR moves into a sizeable surplus in the CUBS forecast in 1985 and 1986 but this is not reflected in lower monetary growth, as the latter is exogenous until 1987. The PSBR effects are translated into an easing of the money growth rate in 1988, however.

3.3 Exogenous assumptions

3.3.1 Introduction

We first describe the various exogenous assumptions. However, this description does not reveal how one forecast differs from another unless the relative importance of each assumption on the different forecasts is known. Accordingly, we then re-compute the forecasts on the basis of a set of common assumptions about the exogenous variables.

The set of common assumptions is generally based on a mean or median value of the various forecast assumptions and is constructed in order to produce a forecast which, together with the published forecast, enables the role of the different exogenous assumptions to be assessed. The common assumptions do not represent any independent view of the role of external or domestic policy developments.

A major problem with defining a set of common exogenous assumptions is that the nature of exogenous variables differs between models. We can distinguish three main differences between models. First, different models may measure an identical concept in different ways. For example, the NIESR and LBS differ in their definition of the price of oil. Here we assume that differences in measurement do not affect forecast developments. Second, some concepts appear in one model but not in any of the others. For example, in the LBS model the world money supply is an exogenous input, but this concept is absent from the other models. Our general approach is to maintain the same relationships, where appropriate, of this variable to the other exogenous inputs. In the case in point, the common assumption definition of the world money supply is assumed to have the same velocity pattern as in the published forecast. Third, we have the exogeneity assumption itself. For example, in most models the PSBR and monetary growth are endogenously determined, whereas they are exogenous inputs in the LPL and CUBS forecasts, respectively. Our practice is to project such exogenous variables in the common assumption framework so that they are consistent with the endogenous outcomes in the other models.

The exogenous assumptions are classified into three groups, relating to the world economy, domestic economic policy, and other areas of the models such as the North Sea sector and the labour market.

3.3.2   World economy assumptions

The first set of assumptions, summarized in Table 3.3, concerns developments in the world economy. The LBS model contains a formal model of the world economy with a larger range of world variables, but the overall system is essentially block-recursive and this sub-system is causally prior to the domestic economy. For the purposes of this exercise variables within this sector are treated as predetermined.

Table 3.3   *Principal exogenous assumptions: world economy*

	1983	1984	1985	1986	1987–90 average	1990–95
			(% per annum)			
World trade						
LBS	–	4.7	5.1	5.0	4.3*	..
NIESR	1.1	4.5	4.8	4.8**	4.9**	..
CE	2.4	5.6	4.3	5.1	3.5	..
CUBS	–0.7	5.8	4.8	4.0	4.2	4.2
LPL	0.3	5.7	6.2	6.2	6.2	6.2
Common assumption	..	5.3	5.0	5.0	4.6	4.9
World wholesale prices ($)						
LBS	6.1	7.0	6.8	7.2	6.8**	..
NIESR	1.4	4.0	4.6	3.4	4.1	..
CE	4.9	11.0	8.9	7.1	7.0	..
CUBS	5.0	5.0	5.0	5.0	5.0	5.0
LPL	5.5	5.0	5.0	5.0	5.0	5.0
Common assumption	..	6.4	6.1	5.5	5.6	5.7
World oil prices ($)						
LBS	–10.7	1.3	9.0	8.2	9.9*	..
NIESR	–7.4	2.0	4.0	4.9**	4.9**	..
CE	–7.9	3.8	4.0	8.3	10.4	..
CUBS	–9.9	5.0	5.0	5.0	5.0	5.0
Common assumption	..	3.0	5.5	6.6	7.6	7.7
World commodity prices ($)						
LBS	4.5	10.5	6.8	7.2	6.0*	..
NIESR	2.0	4.5	4.3	5.4**	5.7**	..
CUBS	5.0	5.0	5.0	5.0	5.0	5.0
Common assumption	..	9.1	5.9	5.9	5.6	5.0

* 1987
** taken from medium-term forecast

The role of the world economy in the various models differs considerably. In the CGP and NIESR models world growth and inflation affect the level of exports and world prices influence the level of imports. In the CGP model the exchange rate is an exogenous variable. In the NIESR model the exchange rate is explained by relative world prices, and interest rates have an influence. The LBS mechanisms are similar to those of the NIESR except that world money supply influences the exchange rate rather than relative prices.

In the CUBS model the growth of world trade enters directly into the equation determining private sector output, while relative prices influence the real exchange rate. The price of world materials, along with world output, influences the determination of domestic prices. In the LPL model world output determines the balance of the volume of trade; however, world prices do not formally enter the model.

The forecasts of world trade show considerably less variation than do the forecasts of domestic output. This may reflect the fact that the assumptions are often based on similar sources. All the models adopt a fairly steady growth assumption, and this is reflected in the common assumption (also shown in Table 3.3), which is based on a simple arithmetic average of the forecasts. Although only the NIESR's short-term forecast is considered, the assumptions used in the medium-term exercise are included in the comparison in order to calculate a set of common assumptions.

The range of forecasts for world inflation (wholesale prices) is somewhat greater than for world trade, with the NIESR adopting a lower rate and CE a somewhat higher rate than the other teams. LPL and CUBS assume a fixed 5 per cent rate of inflation throughout. This assumption is also used by the latter for the forecast in non-oil commodity prices, whereas both NIESR and LBS assume an increasing price of commodities relative to wholesale prices.

With the exception of CUBS, who assume an unchanged ratio of oil prices to wholesale prices throughout, all the teams assume a falling relative price of oil in 1984 with CE having the sharpest fall and NIESR the least. LBS allow for a recovery in the relative price of oil to start in 1985 and CE and NIESR assume that this begins in the following year. The oil price does not enter into the LPL model. Our common assumption forecast assumes a falling relative price in both 1984 and 1985 with an average increase of 2 per cent after 1987.

The world price assumptions in the models are typically expressed in terms of dollars. Since the effective exchange rate declines more sharply in the NIESR and LBS forecasts than the dollar rate, while the two rates move together in the CUBS forecast, the implications for world prices in average currency terms are affected by the particular choice of exogenous assumption.

Foreign interest rates enter only into the LBS, NIESR and LPL models. While the definitions differ, the most important difference is that LPL adopts an exogenous assumption for *real* short and long rates while the others make an assumption for nominal short rates. In their forecast assumptions, however, the real long and short rates differ only marginally. In order to arrive at a common assumption, the nominal assumptions of LBS and NIESR were converted into an equivalent real rate and the consensus real rate was re-calculated as a nominal rate using the consensus forecast of world inflation. The LBS world money supply assumption is re-calculated assuming the same velocity of circulation with respect to world GNP as in the published forecast.

3.3.3   Domestic policy and other assumptions

The models typically do not permit an easy summary of the assumed monetary and fiscal policy stance; this problem is discussed in Chapter 5. Our description of domestic economic policy is in terms of assumptions regarding the appropriate policy instrument. In the LPL model the policy instruments are the tax rate, employers' tax and employees' contributions, the unemployment benefit rate, and the ratio of the PSBR to GDP. The assumptions regarding the tax rate and the PSBR then determine the level of government spending, so that, at least in theory, it is treated endogenously. The model distinguishes between the underlying levels of the PSBR and government spending and the actual levels, which vary according to the cyclical position of the economy. The LPL model further differs from the other models in that its rational expectations framework requires that developments in the terminal year determine government expenditure in the preceding periods.

In all the other models, the level of the PSBR is determined endogenously from given assumptions about the level of taxation and government spending although in setting those assumptions some attention might be paid to the implied PSBR. In the CUBS model the rate of monetary growth is determined exogenously up to 1986 from the MTFS framework, and from then on the money stock grows in proportion to the stock of bonds, which in turn is influenced by the level of the PSBR. Monetary growth is wholly endogenous in the CE, LBS, and NIESR forecasts. The role of interest rates varies greatly between the models. In the LPL model real interest rate differentials are forced to offset the expected gain or loss from real exchange rate changes with nominal interest rates related to the real rate by a Fisher identity. Interest rates do not appear at all in the CUBS model, are exogenous in the CE and NIESR forecasts, and are related to world interest rates in the LBS model.

All the groups model the exchange rate, with the exception of CE, who treat it as predetermined.

The principal assumptions regarding domestic economic policy are shown in Table 3.4. LBS and NIESR assume an unchanged rate of income tax, while the other groups allow for a reduction. In the case of CE and LPL this starts in 1984 and for CUBS in 1987. The common assumption variant assumes a fixed tax rate throughout. All the models assume constant rates of VAT (although the LPL model excludes indirect tax variables). Tax allowances are generally assumed to be inflation-adjusted with the exception of CUBS, where the real value of allowances is increased by an average of 5 per cent per annum between 1983 and 1986 and is then held constant, and where an increase in unemployment benefits is assumed after 1986.

The CE and LBS forecasts assume that the national insurance surcharge (NIS) is removed in 1984, whereas NIESR assume a continuation. CUBS incorporate the surcharge along with employer's contributions and this variable declines in 1985, presumably reflecting the abolition of the NIS. LPL hold employer's contribution rates constant but assume a gradual reduction in the employee's rate. For the purpose of a common assumption, all these rates are held constant.

Assumptions about government expenditure are also shown in Table 3.4. The short-run assumptions for current expenditure are quite similar, with the NIESR a little more expansionary than the rest; but NIESR is more pessimistic in terms of capital expenditure where the LBS is the most expansionary. LBS distinguishes between procurement and employment expenditure while the CUBS assumption relates to the latter. The common assumption path assumes that procurement and employment expenditure grow at the same rate. Government spending is formally endogenized in the LPL forecast by means of forecasting rules. In order to make a roughly equivalent fiscal stance across models, the LPL assumption regarding the ratio of the PSBR to GDP is increased in order to achieve approximately the same PSBR/GDP ratio as the other forecasts. Similarly, the CUBS assumption of base monetary growth (which reflects the centre of the target range of the MTFS) is assumed to be higher in order to match the other assumptions.

The common assumption for interest rates implies a small negative differential between domestic and world rates, compared with the small positive differential in the LBS forecast and the larger negative differential in the NIESR forecast. In principle it would be desirable to standardize domestic interest rates using real rather than nominal rates, as has been done for world interest rates. This would be particularly appropriate when rates of inflation differ considerably between the models. However, whereas a standard assumption regarding world real interest rates can be made by setting an appropriate level of nominal rates given the exogenous assumption for world inflation, domestic inflation is determined endogenously, so it is not possible to set real interest rates in the same way at the domestic level.

The main differences in the assumptions regarding North Sea oil production are largely in respect of how rapidly production achieves its peak level. There is no oil production variable in the LPL model. In the CUBS model an increase in oil production raises the exchange rate directly and lowers the PSBR through higher tax revenues. In the LBS and NIESR models higher oil production also lowers the PSBR and improves the balance of payments. Although the mechanisms differ between these two models, the exchange rate then rises in both cases. The CGP model has no exchange rate reaction so that changes in oil output influence only the PSBR and balance of payments. Although a 10 per cent increase in oil production would, *ceteris paribus*, increase GDP by $\frac{1}{2}$ per cent, the

Table 3.4   *Principal exogenous assumptions: domestic economic policy and North Sea oil*

	1983	1984	1985	1986	1987–90	1990–95
Standard rate of income tax (%)						
CE	30.0	28.5	27.2	26.2	26.2	..
CUBS	30.0	30.0	30.0	30.0	25.0	25.0
LBS	30.0	30.0	30.0	30.0	30.0	..
LPL	30.55	29.7	29.4	28.7	26.8[b]	26.5
NIESR	30.0	30.0	30.0	30.0[d]	30.0[d]	..
Common assumption	30.0	30.0	30.0	30.0	30.0	30.0
Current government expenditure (% p.a.)						
CE	0.5	0.7	0.9	0.8	0.8	..
CUBS	–	0.5	0.5	0.5	1.5	1.5
LBS	1.8	0.3	0.7	0.8	0.8[a]	..
LPL[c]	1.5	–0.2	0.4	0.5	2.1	4.4
NIESR	1.2	1.5	1.1	0.5[d]	0.5[d]	..
Common assumption		0.75	0.75	0.75	1.0	1.5
Government capital expenditure (% p.a.)						
CE	3.3	3.2	3.1	3.0	3.0	..
CUBS	–	2.0	2.0	2.0	2.0	2.0
LBS	4.5	5.4	5.8	3.9	–2.3[a]	..
LPL			(see above)			
NIESR	5.3	0.3	1.0	1.0[d]	1.0[d]	..
Common assumption		2.75	3.0	2.5	1.0	2.0

Standard rate of VAT   All models assume 15% throughout (no variable for LPL)

Employers'/employees' contributions   CUBS and LBS assume a reduction in employers'/NIS contributions; LPL assume a reduction in employees contributions

Rate of unemployment benefit

Constant rate: LBS, LPL; CUBS assume rate rises by 1½% p.a. after 1983

Interest rates						
CE	11.5	11.0	10.5	10.5	10.0	..
LBS (endogenous)	9.2	7.9	7.9	8.0	8.0[a]	..
NIESR		9.5	9.5	..	..	..
Common assumption		9.5	9.3	9.25	9.0	..
Financing						
CUBS: money base growth rate forecast	8.6	7.9	7.0	6.1	..	..
common assumption		10.0	9.2	8.5	..	..
LPL: ratio of PSBR/GDP forecast	0.02	0.02	0.015	0.01	0.01	0.01
common assumption		0.026	0.02	0.018	0.020	0.020
North Sea oil production (% p.a.)						
CE	6.4	7.3	1.7	−2.5	−5.1	−10.7
CUBS	8.7	4.4	–	−7.6	–[a]	..
LBS	7.0	4.8	3.5	–		..
NIESR	8.3	0.8	–	−0.4	..	–
Common assumption		4.3	1.3	−2.6	–	–

a 1987
b 27.5 in 1987, 26.5 in 1988, then constant
c endogenous; current plus capital expenditure
d taken from medium-term forecast

models generally exhibit very little influence on output and employment once full interaction of variables is permitted. In the common assumption forecast, oil production falls in 1986 before stabilizing for the remainder of the forecast horizon.

Forecasts of growth of the working population are quite similar, with the consensus growth being around $\frac{1}{4}$ per cent per annum. The labour supply is endogenous in the CUBS model, while the working population assumption in the LBS case derives from a prior assumption about the population of working age.

3.3.4   Results under common assumptions

Taking the quarterly models first, it is apparent that the effect of adopting common assumptions produces a more subdued recovery in output for the LBS forecast in 1985, with output growth even further depressed in 1986. The effects on inflation are less marked but positive, whereas unemployment is lower (by 300,000 in 1987) despite the lower level of output. The principal changes are higher government expenditure but a higher national insurance surcharge rate. The net effect of changes in the world economy assumptions is to lower export demand, while the lower exchange rate leads to higher inflation and lower real income and consumption.

The common assumptions run also leads to a lower rate of recovery in the NIESR model. Growth over the two years 1984 and 1985 is reduced by $\frac{3}{4}$ per cent while inflation is reduced in 1985. In 1984 most of the effect comes from lower public expenditure growth, while in 1985 lower demand comes principally from lower export growth as the effective exchange rate rises. The effects on unemployment are very small, however.

Turning to the annual models, we find that the effects of the common assumption run on the LPL model is to leave the level of GDP very much unchanged in the short run, although in the longer run it is reduced by $1\frac{1}{2}$ to $1\frac{3}{4}$ per cent. Inflation and unemployment are also very much unchanged in the short run, and over the longer term unemployment remains close to its old level with the price level around 2 per cent higher. The principal differences in exogenous assumptions from the base run are lower world real interest rates and a higher domestic tax rate. Fiscal stance, as measured by the PSBR/GDP ratio, is also assumed to be a little more expansionary, and this accounts for the higher price level in the constant assumption run. The minor change in output in this run is largely explained by the lower real wage ($4\frac{1}{2}$ per cent by 1995) and the higher level of government spending (which goes some way towards offsetting the decline in private spending).

For the CUBS model the set of common assumptions produces a forecast of GDP that is very close to the published forecast in the short term, but there is a deeper decline predicted between 1985 and 1987. By 1990 the level of GDP is 6 per cent lower than in the base forecast with some of this gap narrowed by 1995, when the difference is $5\frac{1}{4}$ per cent. Although GDP is lower throughout, the effects on the level of unemployment vary according to the period considered. By 1988 the level of unemployment is 1.6 million *higher* than in the published or base forecast, attaining a peak of 3.5 million in 1987, so that unemployment is seen to be increasing over this period compared with the decline in the published forecast. After 1989 the unemployment level now declines steadily, so that by 1995 the new level of unemployment is around 0.9 million, 1.1 million lower than in the base forecast. The effects on inflation are even more dramatic. In the short term to 1985 the rate of inflation is some 2 per cent per annum higher than in the base forecast, and between 1985 and 1988 the gap widens to 3 per cent per annum. However, after 1989 the rate of inflation declines, so that by 1992 the price level is *falling* at a rate of 9–10 per cent per annum. These differences in the inflation–unemployment relationship are shown in Figure 3.4, which may be compared with Figure 3.1.

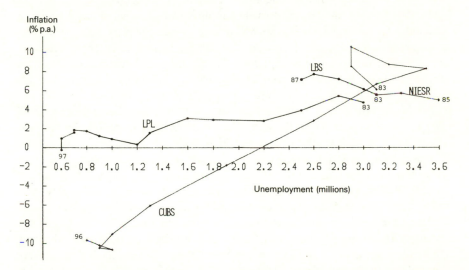

Fig. 3.4   Unemployment–inflation forecasts in the common assumption runs

Another of the striking differences between the common assumption forecast and the base forecast is the behaviour of the exchange rate. The real exchange rate is higher throughout; the nominal exchange rate is lower initially but then more than doubles between 1988 and 1995 to end up 100 per cent higher than in the base forecast.

The dramatic switch in the CUBS forecast runs after 1986–7 is related to the financing assumptions adopted, which move from an exogenous money growth to an endogenous one after 1986. Since bonds are the form of residual finance, and since they have no impact on real or nominal variables elsewhere in the model, whereas money influences prices directly, this switch has important implications for inflation and unemployment. The main differences in the set of exogenous assumptions in the common assumption forecast compared with the base forecast are slightly higher world wholesale prices but lower oil and commodity prices, lower tax allowances, and a higher money base growth rate.

The relative magnitudes of these changed assumptions are as follows. Changed world assumptions lower GDP by $1\frac{3}{4}$ per cent by 1995, raising the level of unemployment by 150,000 and the price level by 6 per cent. The other factor that has a positive impact on prices is the assumption that employers' tax costs remain unchanged. This increases prices by 20 per cent by 1995 and lowers the nominal exchange rate by 17 per cent. These effects on inflation are more than offset by the other changes. Different domestic policy assumptions on expenditure and money base growth lower prices and raise the exchange rate, as does the assumption that the tax rate and real allowances remain constant. By far the most important effect is the assumption that the real unemployment benefit is unchanged; this lowers prices by 30 per cent (by 1995) and raises the exchange rate by 40 per cent while lowering unemployment by 800,000.

In the quarterly models most of the employment differences come from the demand side. In the case of CUBS we are able to see some very different effects from supply and demand factors in the labour market (the labour sector is considered in more detail in Chapter 4). The assumption that real tax allowances stay constant rather than increase in the first few years of the forecast leads to a large reduction of labour supply (1 million persons) but a large part of the effect on unemployment is offset by a reduction in labour demand of $\frac{3}{4}$ million jobs (see Table 3.5). Over the early part of the forecast period the demand effects outweigh the supply influence, which begins to pick up only after 1987. The demand effects largely originate from a rise in the real exchange rate. This in turn comes about as a result of a loss of competitiveness as real wages adjust to the allowance change. The initial effect is to increase labour supply, but subsequently this is reversed as increasing prices lead to lower real wages.

The increase in unemployment resulting from the change in the assumption regarding real unemployment benefits reflects a large (positive) demand effect with only a small offset in the form of lower labour supply. The demand effects themselves are associated with lower prices. A reduction in labour supply also offsets some of the demand effect from the change in the tax rate assumptions, with these effects starting only in 1987 since the tax rate in the base forecast remains constant until then.

The employers' contribution rate changes from the base assumption from 1985 by not falling to a lower level. This is a contribution to the total change where there is an impact effect which flattens out later on. The change in assumptions regarding government expenditure and the money base rate produce a cyclical pattern to GDP. The main influence comes from higher money growth on the price level and the exchange rate.

Overall, re-running the forecasts on common assumptions has little impact on the divergence between the GDP short-term forecasts (1984-5). The average growth of GDP for the four groups examined is now 3 per cent in 1984 followed by 1.8 per cent in 1985, compared with 3 and 2.4 per cent respectively in the

Table 3.5 *Contributions to constant assumptions variant: CUBS model*

		1984	1985	1986	1987	1988	1989	1990	1991	1995
GDP (% differences from base forecast)										
Standard rate of tax		—	—	—	-0.8	-1.5	-2.1	-2.1	-1.7	-1.7
Unemployment benefits		—	—	—	-0.1	-0.1	0.1	0.3	0.3	0.2
Real tax allowances		-0.1	-0.5	-1.3	-2.3	-2.9	-3.0	-2.9	-2.6	-3.0
Employers contributions		—	-0.2	-0.8	-0.6	-0.7	-0.6	-0.4	-0.1	-0.1
Govt. expenditure		0.7	0.7	1.0	0.2	0.2	0.1	-0.1	0.1	0.7
World assumptions		-0.2	-0.2	-0.1	-0.3	-0.6	-0.8	-0.9	-1.3	-1.7
Total		0.4	-0.1	-1.2	-3.8	-5.3	-6.1	-6.1	-5.1	-5.2
Prices (% differences from base forecast)										
Standard rate of tax		—	—	—	-0.8	-1.7	-2.4	-3.3	-6.4	-14.4
Unemployment benefits		—	—	—	-0.3	-1.4	-3.4	-6.5	-14.8	-30.0
Real tax allowances		—	0.1	0.4	-0.8	1.4	1.4	0.5	-4.2	-12.6
Employers contributions		—	—	0.2	1.7	4.2	7.3	10.5	15.2	20.8
Govt expenditure		1.1	3.2	6.1	7.9	8.7	8.0	6.3	1.1	-13.1
World assumptions		0.5	0.3	—	0.2	0.9	1.6	2.3	3.5	6.1
Total		1.7	3.7	6.7	9.7	12.7	13.6	10.7	-6.7	-41.1
Labour demand (d) and supply (s) (thousands)										
Standard rate of tax	(d)	—	—	—	-290	-507	-659	-550		-330
	(s)	—	—	—	-67	-78	-132	-187		-407
Unemployment benefits	(d)	—	—	—	64	202	349	449		688
	(s)	—	—	—	-12	-20	-30	-46		-145
Real tax allowance	(d)	-56	-283	-594	-872	-978	-835	-648		-789
	(s)	9	39	36	-27	-165	-350	-534		-1024
Employers contributions	(d)	—	-172	-356	-439	-420	-313	-199		-145
	(s)	—	-2	-5	-12	-20	-28	-41		-89
Govt expenditure	(d)	25	33	60	38	25	-9	-44		213
	(s)	2	—	-3	-5	-3	-3	-7		-37
World assumptions	(d)	-9	-29	-50	-99	-140	-162	-173		-233
	(s)	9	7	12	12	15	13	5		-67
Total	(d)	-41	-445	-933	-1571	-1874	-1682	-1230		-618
	(s)	16	44	39	-106	-264	-520	-792		-1739

base forecasts. The degree of divergence is actually increased in 1984 and remains unchanged in 1985. Average growth over the following two years (1986–7) is reduced from an average of $1\frac{3}{4}$ to 1 per cent — this is largely attributable to the lower CUBS forecast. The results for the longer-term outlook remain very much unchanged, however.

While the effect on the output forecasts of adopting a set of common assumptions is small, that on the level of unemployment is even less noticeable. The average level of unemployment hardly differs over the period up to 1987 despite the lower average growth of output.

The average of the forecasts for inflation rises by about 1 per cent in both 1984 and 1985 and by about $1\frac{1}{2}$ per cent per annum between 1985 and 1987. There is little narrowing of the divergence between the individual forecasts in 1984, and from 1985 to 1987 the inflation forecasts become more widely spread.

These results are not too surprising when one notes that the differences in the base forecast assumption for world demand, and to some extent world prices, do not differ very much from the common assumption. This probably reflects a certain dependence on similar sources for forecasts of the world economy, e.g. OECD forecasts. Most of the forecasts adopt a similar domestic policy stance so that the main differences in the base forecasts concerning domestic policy revolve around the assumptions about tax rates and employers' contributions, where lower rates are assumed in some of the base forecasts against unchanged levels in the common assumption forecast (but these appear to have little effect on the forecasts). The CUBS reduction in the tax rate does not start until 1987, and if this does not occur growth is lower from then on. The reduction assumed in the LPL base forecast is gradual, but the impact of this change is limited to higher government spending within the confines of a fixed PSBR/GDP ratio.

One interesting feature of the results is that all the forecasts of GDP lie below the path of the published forecasts (see Figure 3.6, which includes other plots to be discussed below). It might be thought that averaging the inputs for a set of approximately linear models would not result in a change in the average output of the models. However, even in the linear case, with different model specifications the average effect on output is not necessarily zero. Moreover, the common assumptions are not simple averages; nor is attention restricted to the forecasts analysed here in setting up the common assumptions. Nevertheless, the persistent downwards tendency is striking, suggesting important asymmetries in the models. (In an earlier exercise we exchanged the exogenous assumptions of the LBS and NIESR forecasts and also observed an asymmetric result, in that the effect on output was negative in *both* models.)

3.4   Residual adjustments

Many of the forecasting teams regularly make residual adjustments to their forecasts (see, for example, Savage, 1983). With a well specified model that is structurally stable, the optimal forecast values of non-autocorrelated equation disturbances are their conditional means of zero (in the absence of any information from stochastic simulations on bias in the deterministic solution). In practice, however, models are not usually well specified and structurally stable, so that recent values of the equation residual may be helpful in forecasting later disturbances. In addition, there are numerous social, political, and economic factors believed to impinge on the model in the forecast period which are not explicitly incorporated in the original specification. Examples might be the announcement of an incomes policy, or direct evidence on the investment intentions of businessmen. In principle, the model should be re-specified to reflect these influences, but the practical approach is more normally to make a set of adjustments to the appropriate relationship in the model. Thus the incomes policy effect might lead to a modification of the wage equations, and the investment intentions evidence might influence the relationship that determines fixed investment.

The introduction of non-zero residuals into the forecasts results in a part of the forecast becoming invariant to other changes in the model, and although they are often referred to as constant adjustments they might also act so as to modify one or more of the slope coefficients. Differences in forecasts between models will therefore reflect differences in the assumptions made regarding the values of these residual adjustments. It is through these adjustments that the skill of the forecaster, as opposed to the quality of the model, appears (or the ingredient of 'tender loving care' is added – Howrey, Klein, and McCarthy, 1974). In order to analyse differences between forecasts we therefore standardize the residual paths adopted in the forecasts.

One of the problems in interpreting the constant-term adjustments in a forecast as purely judgemental effects is that these adjustments or residuals may reflect part of the underlying error process of the structural equations. Osborn and Teal (1979) suggest several alternative mechanical rules for analysing a published forecast. These are: (i) zero adjustment to the equation; (ii) a constant adjustment based on the last four quarters of the pre-forecast period; (iii) constant adjustment based on the last eight quarters; (iv) an autoregressive rule based on simple time series models.

The choice of a constant or a zero residual rule is influenced by several factors. One of these is the ambiguity in selecting a method to derive the value of the non-zero constant (for example (ii) or (iii)). In contrast, the zero residual rule is unambiguous, but may penalize forecasters who use a constant residual as an alternative to revising the intercept of the relevant equation in the model code. Given the frequent use of constant adjustments in the quarterly forecasts considered here, this could be an important issue. The use of a constant value for the equation residual in a system with dynamic effects through lagged dependent variables and/or serially correlated errors implies a cumulative effect on the equation in question. In practice it appears that, given the equation dynamics in the present models, residual rules which produce an overall constant effect on the equation have not been adopted. Thus the projection of many model residuals at a constant value may underestimate their impact on the model forecast. For example, in the LBS model the short-term interest rate residual has a constant value of 0.5 percentage points, but the implicit effect allowing for equation dynamics is 2.5 percentage points by the end of the forecast period.

In this exercise we use examples based on zero residuals, constant residuals, and (in the case of NIESR) autoregressive residuals. For the standard base of comparison we use zero residuals. In using constant residuals a four-quarter average is in fact only used for the quarterly models. In the case of CUBS the equation residual for 1983 is projected forward, and in the absence of this information for the LPL forecast the 1984 level is used. The treatment adopted for the quarterly models glosses over problems of which periods are true pre-forecast periods and which are not: we use the average of the 1983 residuals, yet clearly some of the values used for the fourth quarter are forecast values.

3.4.2   Effects by model

LBS

In the LBS forecast just under 60 endogenous variables are adjusted for all or part of the forecast horizon (these adjustments are published in *Economic Outlook*). Nearly two-thirds of the adjustments are projected to be constant from the 1983(4) level onwards while the remaining one-third either vary in magnitude over the forecast period or apply to only part of the period. In addition there are half-a-dozen or so temporary exogeneity assumptions. Some of the major adjustments are shown in Table 3.6.

Whereas adopting the set of common assumptions reduces output growth and increases inflation, with little impact on unemployment, (see Figure 3.5) setting all the forecast residuals at a level of zero increases growth in 1984 even further (to 4.4 per cent), but subsequent growth is then reduced. Inflation is now very rapid, however, with the price level 10 per cent higher by 1985 and 80 per cent higher by 1987, compared with the published forecast. This result largely occurs as a consequence of removing the earnings residual, which operates so as to provide an increasing reduction on earnings in the published forecast. The zero residual variant produces an unemployment forecast of $2\frac{1}{4}$ million by 1987, half a million lower than in the published forecast. The forecast now implies an inflationary spiral, with the exchange rate falling continuously, provoking accelerating domestic inflation.

The lower exchange rate initially stimulates export growth, but this effect is gradually more than balanced by higher domestic inflation, so that the level of exports falls below that of the published forecast. Higher inflation also results in a higher savings ratio, and this lowers consumer spending despite higher real income. The rise in real incomes is attributable to higher employment as total output rises throughout the first three years of the forecast. The increase in output itself occurs as the removal of a negative residual on fixed investment

Table 3.6 *Major residual adjustments in the LBS forecast*

	Quarter	AEM	KM3L	INPOX	KBJL	M
	1983 (1)	−2.4	−40	−117	2627	−41
	(2)	1.0	153	−248	2000	−
	(3)	−0.6	−57	−150	3000	50
	(4)	−	−	−150	3000	65
Forecast	1984 (1)	−2.5	−	−200	3000	80
	(2)	−2.5	−	−200	4000	95
	(3)	−2.5	−	−200	4000	110
	(4)	−2.5	−	−200	4000	125
	1985 (1)	−3.5	−500	−250	4000	140
	(2)	−3.5	−500	−250	5000	155
	(3)	−3.5	−500	−250	5000	170
	(4)	−3.5	−500	−250	5000	185
	1986 (1)	−4.5	−1000	−275	5000	200
	(2)	−4.5	−1000	−275	6000	200
	(3)	−5.5	−1000	−275	6000	200
	(4)	−5.5	−1000	−275	6000	200
	1987 (1)	−6.5	−1000	−300	6000	200
	(2)	−6.5	−1000	−300	6000	200
	(3)	−7.5	−1000	−300	6000	200
	(4)	−7.5	−1000	−300	6000	200
	1988 (1)	−8.5	−1000	−300	6000	200

Key: AEM−average earnings; KM3L−money stock; INPOX−private non-housing non-oil investment; KBJL−bank lending to persons; M−imports of goods and services.

leads to a rise in investment which more than compensates for lower consumption and export demand.

The earnings adjustment is the most important single adjustment in terms of both output and inflation, and is clearly needed to prevent a strong inflationary effect. The adjustments on imports and investment also have major effects on the output and inflation forecast.

When constant levels of the residuals are used in conjunction with the set of common assumptions (with these residuals given by an average of the values in the four quarters of 1983), the level of output is higher by over 3 per cent by 1987, giving a rapid rate of expansion of output in 1984 and 1985. Inflation is little affected in these two years, but is substantially higher in 1986 and 1987. It is 1985 before the higher level of output has any noticeable effect on the level of unemployment, and by 1987 the level of unemployment is $2\frac{3}{4}$ million as against $2\frac{1}{4}$ million in the published forecast. The sensitivity of productivity in the LBS model comes into play here, with $1\frac{3}{4}$ per cent of the increase in output being absorbed by higher productivity. All this effect occurs in 1984 and arises in the primary and tertiary sector.

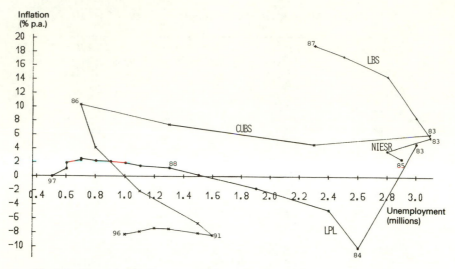

Fig. 3.5   Unemployment–inflation relationships in the common assumptions/zero residuals runs

NIESR

There are 33 non-zero residual adjustments in the NIESR forecast plus some temporary exogeneity assumptions. Fourteen of these adjustments are variable over the forecast horizon with the main ones shown in Table 3.7.

Re-running the NIESR forecast using common exogenous assumptions and zero residual values gives a very rapid rate of recovery of output in 1984, in conjunction with a lower forecast of inflation in both 1984 and 1985. Removal of the negative adjustment to exports and the positive adjustment to imports (see Table 3.7) produces a substantial improvement in net trade. This then leads to an appreciation of the exchange rate relative to the published forecast, which in turn produces a lower rate of domestic inflation. Although there is no longer a positive residual on consumer demand, the effect of lower inflation on the savings ratio more than compensates for this. The published forecast also includes a downward adjustment to stockbuilding in distributive trades, and when this adjustment is removed the improvement in stockbuilding, together with the other increases in final demand described above, induce a higher level of fixed investment. The improved trade position, however, results in an increase in the real exchange rate, so that the beneficial effect on trade wears away over time leaving a peak effect on output in 1984, although the effects on employment and unemployment are not maximized until the end of 1985.

Using instead equation residuals set constant at their average level in the previous four quarters produces a forecast very similar to the published forecast in terms of output growth. There is a switch in the composition of expenditure, however, with lower export, public spending and fixed investment demand

Table 3.7 *Major residual adjustments in the NIESR forecast*

	Quarter		QCND	QDURAB	QXGMA	PXGMA	QDSDT	QMMF
	1983	(1)	42	212	−334	−3.6	−85	531
		(2)	287	177	−395	−1.0	−214	471
		(3)	162	296	−404	−4.5	−100	435
		(4)	−	200	−375	−4.5	−200	450
Forecast	1984	(1)	120	126	−359	−4.5	−125	450
		(2)	−	54	−325	−4.5	−125	450
		(3)	−	28	−300	−4.5	−125	450
		(4)	−	52	−275	−4.5	−125	450
	1985	(1)	−	52	−250	−4.5	−125	450
		(2)	−	52	−250	−4.5	−125	450
		(3)	−	52	−250	−4.5	−125	450
		(4)	−	52	−250	−4.5	−125	450
	1986	(1)	−	52	−250	−4.5	−125	450

Key: QCND−consumers' expenditure on non-durables; QDURAB−consumers' expenditure on durables; QXGMA−volume of exports of manufactures; PXGMA−prices of exports of manufactures; QDSDT−stockbuilding-distributive trades; QMMF−volume of imports of manufactures

balanced by higher consumption growth. The latter arises as a result of a rising exchange rate and its beneficial effect on prices and real incomes. It is also helped by the higher (constant) residual adjustment now applied directly to consumption. Productivity falls as compared with the base forecast, so that employment rises and unemployment falls, but still reaches a level of 3.5 million in 1986.

Finally, we consider a variant in which the residuals in the NIESR forecast are extrapolated mechanically according to regression equations fitted to the sample-period residuals. The general form is a second-order autoregression with an intercept term and a linear time trend, and statistically insignificant co-efficients are set equal to zero. (This is an option available in the NIESR soft-ware.) It results in constant but non-zero residuals in 17 cases, and variable adjustments using the regression equation in 10 cases. Of the residuals shown in Table 3.7, those for stockbuilding and imports are quite similar, while the adjustment for durable consumption is much higher.

The adjustments for export volumes and prices (*QXGMA* and *PXGMA*, respectively) are set equal to zero in the mechanical set of residuals. The fore-cast, when re-run using the set of common assumptions and the residuals generated by the autoregressive method, increases GDP growth substantially compared with both the published forecast and the standard constant residual forecast. In particular, output growth is far more rapid in 1984. This is due to a considerably higher level of exports, which in turn increases the exchange rate through the current balance and thus stimulates real income and consumption demand. However, higher demand also results in higher inflation, particularly in 1985. By then the unemployment level is $3\frac{1}{4}$ million compared with the level of $3\frac{1}{2}$ million in the published forecast.

CUBS
The non-zero adjustments used in the published CUBS forecast (Table 3.8) are a downward adjustment to private sector employment and the nominal exchange rate and upward adjustments to prices and real wages. In the first re-run of the forecast these residuals were set at zero throughout and the common assumptions described earlier were employed. The zero residual variant shows an overall

Table 3.8   *Residual adjustments in the CUBS forecast*

	LEER	LLPR	LTPIM	LQPR	CHRW
1983	−0.0270	−0.040	0.015	−	0.015
1984	−0.0270	−0.035	0.030	0.045	0.010
1985	−0.0270	−0.055	0.030	0.065	0.010
1986	−0.0270	−0.071	−	0.040	−
1987	−0.0270	−0.071	−	−	−
1988	−0.0270	−0.053	−	−	−
1989	−0.0270	−0.053	−	−	−
1990	−0.0270	−0.046	−	−	−
1991	−0.0270	−0.038	−	−	−
1992	−0.0270	−0.038	−	−	−
1993	−0.0270	−0.037	−	−	−
1994	−0.0270	−0.031	−	−	−
1995	−0.0270	−0.025	−	−	−
Constant assumption	−0.0270	−0.040	0.015	−	0.015

Key: LEER−log nominal exchange rate; LLPR−log private sector employment; LTPIM− log price level; LQPR−log private sector output; CHRW−real wage change

reduction in output compared with the published forecast: between 1986 and 1988 the level of output is higher, before falling to a new level which grows in line with that of the published forecast but lies some 4 per cent below it (see Figure 3.6). In the 1990s this level of output is very close to that obtained by using the common exogenous assumptions alone, implying that the effects of the residual adjustments are much weaker towards the end of the forecast horizon. The absence of a negative adjustment to the exchange rate leads both to a higher value for the exchange rate and to lower prices, but most of this effect comes after 1986. Employment demand rises initially as its negative residual is removed, so that unemployment is over 1 million lower in the first four years of the forecast. As the higher real exchange rate reduces output, however, employment demand falls, so that the level of unemployment is higher than in the published forecast between 1989 and 1990. This effect is only temporary as labour supply falls continuously, more than offsetting the labour demand effect.

By 1995 the level of unemployment is over $\frac{1}{2}$ million higher than in the published forecast, reaching a level of just over 1 million persons.

Using constant residuals reduces output from the published forecast by 3 per cent in 1984, building up to 8 per cent by 1995. Forecast growth over the years 1984 and 1985 now averages only $1\frac{3}{4}$ per cent per annum, contrasted with over 4 per cent per annum in the published forecast. The recession originally projected for 1986 no longer occurs (growth actually picks up a little), although there is negligible growth in 1987. Thereafter growth is a steady $1\frac{1}{2}$ per cent per annum ($2\frac{1}{4}$ per cent in the published forecast). The implications for inflation are less marked in the short term, but by 1987 the price level is nearly 17 per cent above the level in the published forecast (11 per cent above the common assumption forecast with the published residual assumptions).

Of all the forecasts, that of CUBS is least affected in the short run by adopting zero residuals. This suggests that the model produces a closer estimate to the actual level for both output and prices in 1983.

LPL

The main residual assumptions in the Liverpool forecast are positive adjustments to inflation, the real exchange rate, and unemployment, and negative effects on government spending and non-durable expenditure. The inflation adjustment is assumed to decline over the period while the unemployment adjustment is phased out by 1987 (see Table 3.9). A negative adjustment to the stock of goods begins in 1986. In a formal representation of the model the inflation rate is given by an identity based on the supply of money and the demand for real money balances, with the former determined by the PSBR/GDP ratio and a

Table 3.9 *Residual adjustments in the LPL forecast*

	G	INFL	RXR	C	EG	RW	U
1984	–	0.095	0.028	−0.03	−0.075	0.010	300
1985	–	0.078	0.020	−0.03	−0.095	–	200
1986	−0.02	0.078	0.010	−0.03	−0.10	–	100
1987	−0.04	0.074	0.015	−0.03	−0.11	–	–
1988	−0.03	0.065	0.010	−0.03	−0.105	–	–
1989	−0.03	0.040	0.005	−0.03	−0.09	–	–
1990	−0.03	0.010	–	−0.03	−0.08	–	–
1991	−0.03	0.010	–	−0.03	−0.07	–	–
1992	−0.03	0.010	–	−0.03	−0.06	–	–
1993	−0.03	0.010	–	−0.03	−0.05	–	–
1994	−0.03	0.010	–	−0.03	−0.05	–	–
1995	−0.03	0.010	–	−0.03	−0.05	–	–
Constant assumption	–	0.095	0.028	−0.03	−0.075	0.01	300

Key: G–stock of durable goods; INFL–inflation rate; RXR–real exchange rate; C–non-durable goods; EG–government spending; RW–real wages; U–unemployment

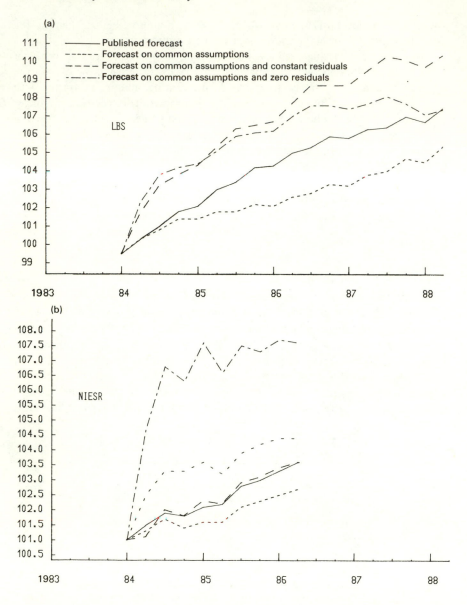

(a)

111 ─── Published forecast
110 ----- Forecast on common assumptions
109 ─ ─ ─ Forecast on common assumptions and constant residuals
     ─·─·─ Forecast on common assumptions and zero residuals

LBS

1983   84   85   86   87   88

(b)

NIESR

1983   84   85   86   87   88

residual. In the operational version of the model, the money supply equation is substituted into the inflation identity, so that the residual appears in this relationship. We interpret the residual as an inflation residual, although it might be described alternatively as a money supply residual that reflects differences in the growth of the nominal money stock from the steady state PSBR/GDP ratio.

Using zero residuals throughout produces some very sharp changes. Some of these obviously reflect the underestimation of output and overestimation of the

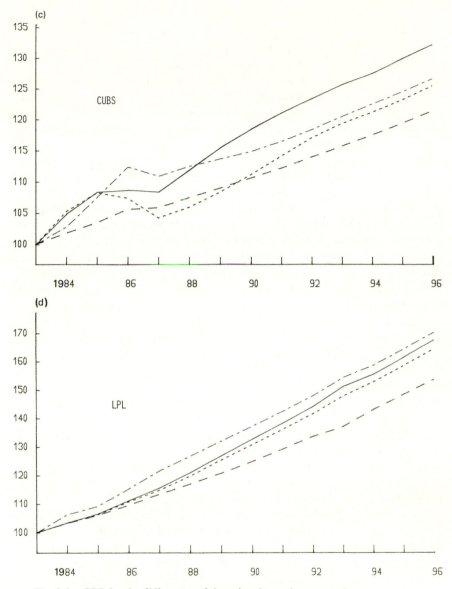

Fig. 3.6   GDP for the different models under alternative assumptions

price level in 1983, but it is noticeable that the price level shows a further substantial decline in 1985. Unemployment remains very much unchanged throughout the forecast, with the level of output consistently above that in the published
forecast (see Figure 3.6). The higher level of output is due to higher non-durable
and government spending. Durable spending and the net trade balance are lower,
the latter as a consequence of the higher real exchange rate. The switch in the

composition of spending comes from price expectations and hence nominal interest rates.

The effects of keeping the adjustments constant at their 1984 levels produces a substantial effect on output in the medium-to-long term. By 1995 GDP is $8\frac{1}{2}$ per cent lower than in the published forecast and $6\frac{1}{2}$ per cent of this is attributable to the residual assumptions. By 1990 the level of unemployment is 1.2 million higher than in the published forecast, averaging well over 2 million. Inflation is also higher, with the price level increased by $7\frac{1}{4}$ per cent in 1984 and $11\frac{1}{2}$ per cent by 1990.

There are no major changes in the Liverpool forecast when the common assumptions are employed. The use of constant residuals has a more marked effect on the forecast of output, unemployment and inflation. A large part of the output change is due to the real exchange rate residual, and the inflation residual influences the low levels of unemployment and inflation in the published forecast. Using zero residuals gives some very striking results for inflation. The published forecast therefore appears to be very dependent on the assumption regarding the inflation residual. The model alone would clearly produce unrealistic forecasts of the inflation rate in the short term, and the longer-term outlook for unemployment is conditional on this residual declining over the forecast horizon. The influence of the residuals illustrates the nature of the terminal condition for inflation in the LPL model. This is set at zero and is effectively reset by the value of the inflation residual.

3.4.3   Effects on the distribution of forecasts

A summary of the results is given in Table 3.10 and the effects on GDP illustrated in Figure 3.6. Earlier it was noted that the use of common assumptions alone does not reduce the divergence of the forecasts of output, inflation, and unemployment, although it does lower the average growth of output between 1983 and 1985 and increase the expected rate of inflation between 1983 and 1987. In fact, the divergence of the output forecasts in 1984 is increased by using the set of common assumptions.

Using constant residual adjustments throughout in addition to the set of common assumptions leads to a reduction in average growth and an increase in average inflation compared with the published forecasts, but with little impact on unemployment in the short term. The average of the four published GDP growth forecasts for 1984 and 1985 is $5\frac{1}{2}$ per cent. Using common assumptions about the exogenous variables brings this down to $4\frac{3}{4}$ per cent. Adopting a constant residual path in addition does not lead to any further total reduction but changes the distribution of growth between the years. The divergence of the output forecasts is in fact narrowed slightly in 1984 and 1985, with a 'low' of 1.8 per cent growth now 'forecast' by CUBS in 1984 against the 'high' of LBS of nearly 4 per cent. Thus the ranking of forecasts by output growth completely reverses the position of CUBS and LBS. A similar movement in these relative positions also occurs in 1985. In 1986-7 the average forecast growth rises from

Table 3.10 *Forecasts of output, inflation, and unemployment under various assumptions*

	1984	1985	1986–87	1988–90	1991–95
GDP (% p.a.)					
LBS					
Published forecast	1.9	2.4	1.6	..	..
Common assumptions (CA)	1.7	1.0	1.0	..	..
CA and constant residuals	3.9	2.8	2.1	..	..
CA and zero residuals	4.4	2.1	1.5	..	..
NIESR					
Published forecast	2.0	1.0	..	..	..
Common assumptions (CA)	1.7	0.6	..	..	..
CA and constant residuals	2.0	1.1	..	..	..
CA and zero residuals	6.6	0.9	..	..	..
CA and mechanical residuals	3.4	0.7	..	..	..
CUBS					
Published forecast	4.9	3.3	–	3.0	1.9
Common assumptions (CA)	5.3	2.9	−3.7	2.2	2.1
CA and constant residuals	1.8	1.7	1.1	1.4	1.5
CA and zero residuals	4.6	4.6	–	1.2	1.7
LPL					
Published forecast	3.5	3.0	4.1	4.7	4.0
Common assumptions (CA)	3.4	2.8	3.9	4.4	3.9
CA and constant residuals	3.2	2.7	3.4	3.2	3.5
CA and zero residuals	6.4	2.7	5.5	4.1	3.7
Inflation (% p.a.)					
LBS					
Published forecast	5.9	6.3	7.2	..	..
Common assumptions	6.1	7.2	7.4	..	..
CA and constant residuals	5.3	7.5	12.0	..	..
CA and zero residuals	8.5	14.4	18.1	..	..
NIESR					
Published forecast	5.8	6.1	..	..	..
Common assumptions	5.7	5.0	..	..	..
CA and constant residuals	5.5	5.2	..	..	..
CA and zero residuals	3.6	2.5	..	..	..
CA and mechanical residuals	6.0	7.5	..	..	..
CUBS					
Published forecast	6.8	8.3	5.6	2.2	2.9
Common assumptions	8.5	10.5	8.5	2.6	−9.3
CA and constant residuals	7.3	9.9	10.8	3.4	0.4
CA and zero residuals	7.4	10.3	1.0	−7.7	−7.9
LPL					
Published forecast	3.4	2.1	0.7	−0.6	−0.4
Common assumptions	5.4	3.9	2.9	1.6	1.4
CA and constant residuals	10.6	8.7	9.5	10.0	9.7
CA and zero residuals	−10.1	−4.8	−0.7	1.5	2.8
Unemployment (millions)					
LBS					
Published forecast	3.1	3.0	2.9	..	..
Common assumptions	3.0	2.8	2.6	..	..
CA and constant residuals	3.0	2.7	2.4	..	..
CA and zero residuals	3.0	2.8	2.4	..	..

Table 3.10 (*cont.*)

	1984	1985	1986–87	1988–90	1991–95
NIESR					
Published forecast	3.1	3.6	..	..	..
Common assumptions	3.3	3.6	..	..	..
CA and constant residuals	3.2	3.5	..	..	..
CA and zero residuals	2.8	2.9	..	..	..
CA and mechanical residuals	3.0	3.2	..	..	..
CUBS					
Published forecast	2.8	2.4	2.2	1.5	1.9
Common assumptions	2.9	2.9	3.4	2.5	1.0
CA and constant residuals	3.0	2.9	3.0	3.1	2.9
CA and zero residuals	2.3	1.3	0.8	1.4	1.3
LPL					
Published forecast	2.8	2.6	2.0	1.3	0.7
Common assumptions	2.8	2.5	2.0	1.4	0.8
CA and constant residuals	2.6	2.5	2.4	2.4	2.0
CA and zero residuals	2.7	2.3	1.7	1.1	0.6

the published figures as a result of higher CUBS and LBS forecasts outweighing the reduction in output growth in the LPL forecast. Over the longer term (1988–95) both CUBS and LPL forecasts are lower than in the published forecasts by about 1 per cent per annum.

A zero residual rule *increases* output growth initially, with an average forecast of $5\frac{1}{2}$ per cent for 1984 alone and over 8 per cent for 1984 and 1985 together. The divergence of the forecasts is narrowed in 1984 with a 'low' of 4.4 per cent for LBS and a 'high' of 6.6 per cent for NIESR. For 1985 however there is no such narrowing of the spread of the output forecasts, with CUBS now the most optimistic ($4\frac{1}{2}$ per cent) and NIESR the most pessimistic (1 per cent) of the forecasts. The impact on inflation is quite dramatic, with a low of -10 per cent for LPL in 1984 and a high of $8\frac{1}{2}$ per cent for 1985 for LBS.

The very big differences between estimates of growth and inflation under zero residuals for 1984 against the published forecasts reflect the varying degrees of success in estimating the *level* of output and prices in the base year. Over the short term the CUBS forecast is the least sensitive to this residual assumption.

The (small) reduction in the spread of forecasts emerging under the common assumptions/standard residual forecasts is due entirely to the latter change. The common assumptions variant alone leads to an increase in the range of the output forecasts.

One of the interesting issues in these comparisons is the smaller variation in forecasts of unemployment and the relative lack of sensitivity of unemployment to changes in the output forecast.

Inspection of Figure 3.6 suggests that the zero-residual-based forecasts of GDP tend to be closer to the published forecast level of GDP by the end of the forecast horizon than do the constant-residual-based estimates, but further away in the short term. This suggests that the role of the residual assumption may be less important as the forecast develops. In order to verify this, we now divide the forecast differences into three categories.

3.5 Decomposition of forecasts

In this section we break down the difference of each forecast from the average of all the forecasts into component parts: differences in exogenous assumptions, differences in judgemental factors (i.e. the effect of the residuals), and differences in the models. The last is defined as the balancing item after calculating the parts of the forecast differences arising from the first two. To the extent that there are problems in defining exactly comparable sets of exogenous variables and residuals, the allocation of the remainder to model differences can only be very approximate.

The various contributions are measured in the following way. Let P be the published model forecast of a variable and let A be the average of the published forecasts of this variable. Then $P - A$ is the total difference to be explained. If CA is the model forecast based on the set of common exogenous assumptions, then the contribution of the exogenous variables to the forecast difference is $P - CA$. If CAR is the model forecast using both common exogenous assumptions and the chosen residual paths, then the contribution of the residuals is $CA - CAR$. The difference in the published forecast from the average owing to model difference is therefore defined as $CAR - A$. After 1989 the comparison is only between CUBS and LPL.

Two sets of decompositions are shown. The first (Table 3.11) uses the zero residual variant, whereas the second (Table 3.12) uses a constant residual path. Inspection of Table 3.11, the zero residual case, suggests that the role of the exogenous assumptions in explaining forecast differences is relatively small but perhaps more important over the longer time span. Only in the case of LBS (in 1985) and CUBS (in 1995) do the exogenous assumptions explain more than one-quarter of the forecast difference in GDP. The size of the exogenous effects is greater in the case of the price forecasts but, with the exception of CUBS, small relative to the other contributions. Thus, the balance of the differences in forecasts is explained in an accounting sense by the role of the residuals and of the model. In most cases these contributions are large and offsetting. The smallest absolute effects, although still offsetting, are for the CUBS forecast of GDP.

For the other three models the residuals consistently act so as to produce a lower forecast level of GDP, with the largest effects in the NIESR forecast. There are indications that the size of the residual contribution diminishes as the forecast period lengthens.

For the price forecasts the role of the residuals in the LBS forecast is to lower the price level, whereas the reverse is the case for the other models. The largest effects appear for LPL. The importance of the exogenous assumptions rises over time for the price forecasts and this may be due to the cumulative effect on the price level from the assumption of a given inflation rate.

Table 3.11 *Decomposition of forecasts: zero residual assumptions**

	Total difference^a			Contribution of exogenous variables^b			Contribution of residuals^c			Contribution of model^d		
	1984	1985	1995	1984	1985	1995	1984	1985	1995	1984	1985	1995
						(% of average forecast)						
GDP forecasts												
LBS	−1.1	−1.1	..	0.3	1.7	..	−2.7	−3.7	..	1.2	0.9	..
NIESR	−1.1	−2.4	..	0.2	0.6	..	−4.6	−4.9	..	3.3	1.8	..
CUBS	1.8	2.7	−10.8	−0.4	0.1	4.6	2.4	0.8	−0.9	−0.3	1.8	−14.5
LPL	0.3	1.0	10.8	0.1	0.2	2.0	−2.9	−2.5	−2.0	3.1	3.3	10.8
Price forecasts												
LBS	0.4	1.0	..	−0.2	−1.0	..	−2.5	−9.3	..	3.1	11.3	..
NIESR	0.3	0.7	..	−	1.1	..	2.0	4.3	..	−1.7	−4.7	..
CUBS	1.3	3.7	21.3	−1.7	−3.9	49.8	3.7	6.8	16.5	−0.7	0.9	−45.0
LPL	−1.9	−5.3	−21.3	−1.9	−3.6	−21.3	15.5	22.5	25.8	−15.4	−24.1	−25.7

* Components may not sum to totals owing to rounding.
a The difference between the published forecast and the average of all the forecasts expressed as a percentage of the average forecast
b That part of the total difference resulting from a comparison of the published forecast with the common assumption forecast
c That part of the total difference resulting from a comparison of the common assumption forecast with the forecast based on common assumptions and the selected residual variant
d The remaining part of the total difference

Table 3.12 *Decomposition of forecasts: constant residual assumptions**

	Total difference[a]			Contribution of exogenous variables[b]			Contribution of residuals[c]			Contribution of model[d]		
	1984	1985	1995	1984	1985	1995	1984	1985	1995	1984	1985	1995
				(% of average forecast)								
GDP forecasts												
LBS	−1.1	−1.1	..	0.3	1.7	..	−2.2	−4.0	..	0.7	1.2	..
NIESR	−1.1	−2.4	..	0.2	0.6	..	−0.2	−0.7	..	−1.1	−2.3	..
CUBS	1.8	2.7	−10.8	−0.4	0.1	4.6	3.4	4.7	2.6	−1.2	−2.0	−18.0
LPL	0.3	1.0	10.8	0.1	0.2	2.0	0.2	0.3	7.1	0.1	0.4	1.7
Price forecasts												
LBS	0.4	1.0	..	−0.2	−1.0	..	0.6	0.4	..	−	1.6	..
NIESR	0.3	0.7	..	−	1.1	..	−	−	..	0.3	−0.3	..
CUBS	1.3	3.7	21.3	−1.7	−3.9	49.8	1.2	1.8	−54.1	1.9	5.9	25.6
LPL	−1.9	−5.3	−21.3	−1.9	−3.6	−21.3	−4.9	−9.6	−133.0	5.0	8.0	133.0

* Components may not sum to totals owing to rounding.
[a] The difference between the published forecast and the average of all the forecasts expressed as a percentage of the average forecast
[b] That part of the total difference resulting from a comparison of the published forecast with the common assumption forecast
[c] That part of the total difference resulting from a comparison of the common assumption forecast with the forecast based on common assumptions and the selected residual variant
[d] The remaining part of the total difference

Using constant residuals (Table 3.12) can, by definition, only change the balance of the contributions of the residuals and the model. With constant residuals the roles of the residuals and the model now often operate in the same direction in contrast to the zero residual case, where they are generally off-setting. The absolute size of the residual and model effects are typically weaker than for the zero residual variant, and there is not the same weakening of the contributions of the residuals over time. One conclusion from these results is that the role of the residuals in the forecast is to bring the model on track in the early part of the forecast period rather than permanently to modify the model. However, in some cases the residual assumptions do clearly affect the long-term development of the forecast.

The LBS forecast is relatively pessimistic both in terms of output and inflation. The influence of the residuals is most important for the output forecast with partially offsetting effects from the exogenous assumptions (quite important in 1985) and the model. In contrast to the output results, the role of the residuals in the inflation forecast is one of lowering prices, and although the contribution of the exogenous assumption operates in the same direction, the model effect is dominant in increasing prices. There is little difference between the relative roles of the three influences on the forecast of GDP when the residuals are assumed to be constant, but the residuals and model effects now work together in explaining the difference in the price forecast.

In the NIESR forecast the lower level of GDP relative to an average of the forecasts is due largely to the effects of the residuals, as both the exogenous variables and the model are such as to increase output. In the price forecast the higher level of prices relative to the other forecasts is also explained in an accounting sense by the residuals, but here the exogenous assumptions play a supporting role. Using constant residuals would attribute the major influence in explaining the forecast differences in output and prices to the model, with fairly weak supporting effects from the residuals.

The LPL forecast is relatively optimistic in terms of output and inflation in the short term and more optimistic than CUBS in the longer term. This result is largely a product of the model, since the residual adjustments are such as to lower output and increase prices. The residual effect diminishes substantially over time, however. Using constant residual adjustments would attribute an opposite role to the residuals. They then act to increase the level of output and to lower prices, in the former case augmenting the influence of the model. Unlike the zero residual variant, there is no sign of a diminishing residual influence over time. The assumptions regarding the terminal conditions and the year in which they appear is quite crucial to the LPL forecast. No sensitivity analysis of the forecast with respect to these terminal conditions has been conducted here, but they clearly introduce an element of judgement absent in the other forecasts.

Finally, we consider the other annual model, that of CUBS. Here the output forecast is relatively optimistic in the short term but more pessimistic than LPL in the longer run. The price forecast is relatively pessimistic throughout. The role of the model is small relative to the other forecasts in terms of the price forecast in the short term, but the role of the exogenous variables in explaining forecast differences in the price level is fairly substantial. In general, the CUBS forecast seems less sensitive to residual adjustments than the other forecasts.

3.6 Summary and conclusions

In this exercise a set of published forecasts made in late 1983/early 1984 from four groups (CUBS, LBS, LPL, and NIESR) have been compared. The published forecasts themselves reveal a considerable diversity. The two annual models (CUBS and LPL) are more optimistic about short-term output growth, with subsequent implications for the level of unemployment, than either of the two quarterly models, with LPL also being much more optimistic about inflation trends than the other groups. Allowing for differences in assumptions about major exogenous variables does not reduce the divergence of the forecasts from each other; rather, it tends to increase it slightly. A more important factor behind the spread of forecasts appears to be the role of judgement as embodied in assumptions about the projected equation residuals. Nevertheless, after standardization of these residuals, there still remains a considerable divergence in forecasts across models, thus tending to confirm the importance of the models themselves as a major cause of forecasting differences.

One broad conclusion is that the role of the exogenous assumptions in explaining forecast differences is quite small. Allocation of the remaining contribution to forecast differences between the influence of the residuals and that of the model is dependent on the rule adopted for the residuals. The results from using the zero residual rule support the proposition that the role of the residuals is to bring the model back on track at the start of the forecast period. However, in several cases the residuals also have an important effect in the development of the forecast.

Some qualifications to the results need to be made. Problems in selecting a set of common assumptions that corresponds with the extraneous information set of each model introduce an element of uncertainty into the allocation of differences between the published forecast and common assumption runs to differences in the exogenous inputs. The existence of alternative standardization rules for the residual adjustments introduces a note of uncertainty into the allocation of forecast differences to judgement. However, the fact that this is the second study to have concluded that the role of exogenous factors in explaining forecast differences is relatively small is worthy of emphasis.

One potential reason for the minor role of exogenous influences is the similar broad assumption adopted for monetary and fiscal policy stance. What is not clear is the extent to which the particular choice of policy instruments has been influenced by the results of earlier forecast runs. A formal policy optimization framework is apparently not employed in short-term and medium-term forecasting exercises. Whether or not implicit policy optimization occurs in the iterative development of a forecast is an open question.

We have examined a single forecast round. Further replications of the study would be needed in order to make general statements regarding forecast differences. No attempt has been made to evaluate the forecasts, although the passage of time and appropriate archiving will enable *ex post* analysis to be undertaken at some future date.

Chapter 4

The Treatment of the Labour Market

4.1 Introduction

This chapter has two main aims. It seeks to clarify and contrast the labour market sectors of the six UK models; it also aims to examine the links between these models and more general evidence on the labour market. It is hoped that this will help to stimulate a more general interest in macroeconomic models and their structure, and to encourage academic research to focus on issues pertinent to macroeconomic models.

Chapters 2 and 3 have revealed the importance of the labour market for the overall properties of the models. One important issue is whether a labour market actually exists within a given model, and if so, how it behaves. A general framework for analysis is set out in Section 4.2, and whether labour markets can be classified as market-clearing or non-market-clearing is considered. The main finding is that many of the model structures are not built around the concept of a market, and labour demand, labour supply, and wages are often modelled in a way that leaves the underlying market structure ill-defined. Symptomatic of this lack of structure is the frequent allocation of wage equations to the 'wage–price' sector rather than to their rightful place, the labour market.

The individual components are considered in the sections that follow. Thus, Sections 4.3, 4.4, and 4.5 deal in turn with labour demand, labour supply, and wage determination. There are two models, namely CUBS and LPL, in which the concept of a labour market is clear and which thereby permit an examination of some of the features of the labour market system as a whole; this is done in Section 4.6. Concluding comments are contained in Section 4.7.

In this chapter attention is concentrated on the economic issues that surround the modelling of the labour market, whether or not this is undertaken in the context of a complete macroeconomic model. Detailed questions of the statistical performance of the equations, econometric methodology, goodness-of-fit, and so forth are in general left on one side.

4.2 General overview

4.2.1 A framework for analysis

Competing views of the operation of the aggregate labour market are characterized by the speed at which the real wage moves to clear the market. The market-clearing or 'equilibrium' view has the real wage adjusting instantaneously; the non-market-clearing or 'disequilibrium' version less quickly, if at all. The implications for both employment and unemployment differ. In the former employment coincides with the planned labour supply and labour demand decisions of agents, and any unemployed individuals are not working because they choose not to do so at the prevailing real wage. In the latter some plans are frustrated, and if these relate to labour supply, then individuals are (involuntarily) unemployed because they are unable to find work at the prevailing real wage. (The equilibrium view may also accommodate a measure of frictional and search unemployment.)

In order to formalize these notions, and to identify key distinctions, consider the following simple model of the aggregate labour market:

$$n_t^s = \delta_1 W_t + \delta_2 Z_t^s \tag{1}$$

$$n_t^d = -\alpha_1 W_t + \alpha_2 Z_t^d \tag{2}$$

where n_t^s is labour supply, n_t^d is labour demand, W_t is the real wage (or their logarithms), and Z_t^s and Z_t^d are vectors of exogenous variables respectively influencing supply and demand. The possibility that taxes drive a wedge between suppliers' and demanders' relative price may be taken account of in Z^s, Z^d under a suitable re-parameterization. Lagged employment (which is *not* necessarily lagged supply or lagged demand) and lagged real wage terms may also appear in Z^s, Z^d.

The market-clearing real wage, denoted W_t^*, is the solution to (1) and (2) given

$$n_t^s = n_t^d = n_t \tag{3}$$

namely

$$W_t^* = (\alpha_1 + \delta_1)^{-1}(\alpha_2 Z_t^d - \delta_2 Z_t^s). \tag{4}$$

The corresponding reduced form for employment is

$$n_t^* = (\alpha_1 + \delta_1)^{-1}(\alpha_2 \delta_1 Z_t^d + \alpha_1 \delta_2 Z_t^s). \tag{5}$$

If for some reason (3) does not apply, so that W_t^* is not attained, then, by rearranging (1) and (2), we observe that

$$W_t - W_t^* = (\alpha_1 + \delta_1)^{-1}(n_t^s - n_t^d). \tag{6}$$

This simply associates a real wage higher than its market-clearing level with an excess supply of labour, and vice versa.

In the absence of market-clearing we have as yet no explanation of how employment is determined, nor of how the real wage adjusts to excess supply or demand. A popular general specification for the wage adjustment is the error correction mechanism (ECM), namely:

$$W_t - W_{t-1} = \beta_1(W_t^* - W_{t-1}^*) + \beta_2(W_{t-1}^* - W_{t-1}) + \beta_3 Z_t^w. \tag{7}$$

This reduces to the partial adjustment model if the restriction $\beta_1 = \beta_2$ is imposed:

$$W_t - W_{t-1} = \beta_2(W_t^* - W_{t-1}) + \beta_3 Z_t^w. \tag{8}$$

The variables Z_t^w represent any institutional or administered features that may tend to keep the real wage away from its market-clearing level. Neglecting these for the moment, we see that both (7) and (8) have the static equilibrium solution $W = W^*$, which is attained provided the adjustment parameter, β_2, is positive; if $\beta_2 = 1$ there is instantaneous adjustment, or market-clearing.

Eliminating W_t^* between (6) and (7), we obtain

$$W_t - W_{t-1} = \frac{\beta_1 \{(n^d - n^s)_t - (n^d - n^s)_{t-1}\} + \beta_2(n^d - n^s)_{t-1}}{(a_1 + \delta_1)(1 - \beta_1)} + \frac{\beta_3 Z_t^w}{1 - \beta_1} \quad (9)$$

which reduces, if $\beta_1 = \beta_2$, to

$$W_t - W_{t-1} = \frac{\beta_2(n_t^d - n_t^s)}{(\alpha_1 + \delta_1)(1 - \beta_2)} + \frac{\beta_3 Z_t^w}{1 - \beta_2} \quad (10)$$

The lagged excess demand terms arise in (9), but not in (10), because of the presence of W_{t-1}^* in the ECM. Although (9) is more general, we concentrate on the partial adjustment equation in the following discussion. Equation (10) exhibits a close resemblance to the expectations augmented Phillips curve (APC),

$$w_t - w_{t-1} = -\lambda_1 U_t + \lambda_2(p_t^e - p_{t-1}) + \lambda_3 Z_t^w \quad (11)$$

where U_t is some measure of unemployment, w_t is the (log) nominal wage level, p_t is the (log) nominal price level, $W_t = w_t - p_t$, $p_t^e = E(p_t|I_{t-1})$, and I_{t-1} is some information set available in the last period. In the special case where

(i) $\lambda_2 = 1$ (homogeneity)
(ii) $p_t^e = p_t$ (perfect foresight)
(iii) U_t is a good proxy for $-(n^d - n^s)_t$,

(11) reduces to (10). Thus one interpretation of the APC is that it is a non-homogeneous version of a non-market-clearing wage adjustment equation. Next, if we add to (11) a target real wage, $\hat{W}_t$, and a lagged real-wage term, we obtain the real-wage resistance hypothesis (RWR):

$$w_t - w_{t-1} = -\lambda_1 U_t + \lambda_2(p_t^e - p_{t-1}) + \lambda_3 Z_t^w + \lambda_4 \hat{W}_t + \lambda_5 W_{t-1}. \quad (12)$$

The inclusion of the target real wage is based on the loose notion that bargaining between employees and employers has an effect on the path of nominal wages and prices through time (Sargan, 1964). The lagged real-wage term adds further dynamics. The crucial issue for both (11) and (12) is homogeneity, and this is clearly a testable proposition. Although the simple *ad hoc* adjustment specified earlier necessarily implies homogeneity, we note that richer theories of wage determination which stress the non-competitive nature of the labour market may exhibit non-homogeneity, at least in the short run. Nominal wage rigidity could arise because workers are locked into wage contracts. Also, the possibility that (iii) may not be true is often thought to be one reason why the Phillips curve has performed badly when confronted by the data; Wadhwani (1982) suggests that better proxies may be available. Finally, it would be wrong to associate the Phillips curve uniquely with non-market-clearing models; theoretical market-clearing contributions have been made by Friedman (1968), Phelps (1967, 1970), and Mortensen (1970), and the empirical work of Lucas and Rapping (1969) is of this school.

Using (1) and (2) to substitute for the endogenous excess demand term in (10) yields the reduced form

$$W_t - (1 - \beta_2)W_{t-1} = \beta_2(\alpha_1 + \delta_1)^{-1}(\alpha_2 Z_t^d - \delta_2 Z_t^s) + \beta_3 Z_t^w. \tag{13}$$

Comparing with the equilibrium reduced form, equation (4), we observe that (4) nests within (13), by setting $\beta_2 = 1$ (and $\beta_3 = 0$). If $\beta_2 = 0$, then W_t follows a first-order difference equation with a unit root. The evidence supplied by Altonji and Ashenfelter (1980) may be interpreted as supporting this latter hypothesis.

In a non-market-clearing model further assumptions are required to determine employment. For the purposes of classifying the modelling teams a simple framework will suffice. Suppose that employment, n_t, is a weighted average of supply and demand,

$$n_t = (1 - \Phi_t)n_t^d + \Phi_t n_t^s \qquad\qquad 0 < \Phi_t < 1. \tag{14}$$

A model developed by Hansen (1970) and Muellbauer (1978), *inter alia*, to explain the coexistence of aggregate vacancies and unemployment posits a large number, N, of micro-markets, some of which are in excess supply and some of which are in excess demand. If the underlying density function generating these N observations is normal, then in (14) Φ_t is the cumulative normal distribution of the standardized variable $(n^s - n^d)/\sigma$, and therefore can be interpreted as the proportion of markets in excess demand. This is demonstrated to be an employment equation suitable for estimation by Nickell (1980), and Kooiman and Kloek (1979). A third term occurs, which reduces the level of aggregate employment the greater the underlying population variance. This can be interpreted as a frictional effect which would disappear with only one market. This latter case is typical of many models, whence Φ_t becomes a binary variable, and (14) becomes the familiar 'min' condition. Under market-clearing, (14) reduces to (3).

Within this framework we should be able to characterize any of the modelling teams' labour markets. Or should we? A common approach to modelling the labour market is to estimate a demand equation and a wage equation. In a market-clearing model this corresponds to (2) and (4), which is the same as the structures (1) and (2) provided recognition is made of any over-identifying restrictions. (If Z_t^s and Z_t^d are distinct scalars the model is just identified.) A demand equation and a wage equation in non-market-clearing corresponds to (2) and any of the wage adjustment equations. (The implicit assumption is that of excess supply, i.e. $\Phi_t = 0$ in (14).) If the reduced-form wage equation (13) is chosen, then the similarity between this and the market-clearing reduced form (4) is striking. The lagged real wage in (13) is the key distinction, giving the disequilibrium wage model its sluggishness. However, if either the supply equation or the demand equation contains the lagged real wage (Andrews, 1983; Symons, 1982), then we face a clear observational equivalence problem. For example, let

$$n_t^s = \delta_1 W_t + \delta_3 W_{t-1} + \delta_2 Z_t^s$$

$$n_t^d = -\alpha_1 W_t + \alpha_2 Z_t^d$$

be the two structural equations. The market-clearing real wage is given by

$$W_t^* = (\alpha_1 + \delta_1)^{-1} (\alpha_2 Z_t^d - \delta_2 Z_t^s) - \delta_3 (\alpha_1 + \delta_1)^{-1} W_{t-1}$$

and the disequilibrium wage under the partial adjustment hypothesis (13), assuming for the moment that $\beta_3 = 0$, by

$$W_t = \beta_2 (\alpha_1 + \delta_1)^{-1} (\alpha_2 Z_t^d - \delta_2 Z_t^s) + [1 - \beta_2 \{1 + \delta_3 (\alpha_1 + \delta_1)^{-1}\}] W_{t-1}.$$

Suppose that one of the above plus the demand equation is estimated. If market-clearing is the implicit structure, then the five underlying parameters can be recovered, whereas the six underlying parameters for non-market-clearing cannot. More generally, Z_t^d and Z_t^s are vectors, and so the only possible difference between the two models is the different degree of over-identification. The problem arises because the reader is presented with estimates of (quasi-) reduced forms. Clearly, if the structure is estimated directly then a test of $\beta_2 = 1$ can be performed, as well as a test of the validity of the over-identifying restrictions. In principle, there is further information contained in Z^w, which we have ignored by setting $\beta_3 = 0$. In practice, such information may be of little use. First, institutional features are often measured only by dummy variables. Second, the same Z^w variables that would occur in the wage adjustment equation occur in labour supply if the structure is market-clearing (the replacement ratio or union 'power' are cases in point).

The implications for unemployment differ markedly between the two structures. Whereas in both structures we may postulate that unemployment consists of those members of the labour force not working,

$$U_t = L_t - n_t \tag{15}$$

where L_t is the labour force, the distinction arises in that some of the unemployed may wish to work, but cannot. By rewriting (15) as

$$U_t = L_t - n_t^s + (n_t^s - n_t) \tag{16}$$

and noting that $n_t = n_t^d$ whether excess supply or market-clearing, then a suitable generalization is obtained. The last term measures involuntary unemployment and is precisely zero in the market-clearing structure. The key problem is in modelling the labour force, L_t. It is in this area that more information can be obtained from cross-section and panel data. Indeed, this rich source of information has been of great use in our understanding of labour supply, where sensible time series models are relatively rare. We return to this question in Section 4.4.

In the light of this general framework, we now proceed to examine the various models.

4.2.2   A brief description of each model

NIESR's labour market contains employment and wage equations. Total employment is broken into four different categories: (i) manufacturing, (ii) mainly public industries, (iii) other industries, and (iv) public administration and defence. In (iv), employment is determined as a fixed proportion of output; in the other three, employment is demand-determined as in (2). Unemployment is determined as the difference between an exogenous labour force and employment, assuming a 5 per cent non-registration rate of those who are unemployed. The key equation in the determination of incomes is an equation for the growth in wage rates, which takes the form of the RWR as in (12). It exhibits homogeneity in the long run but not in the short run.

The next two models, LBS and HMT, possess wage equations that are of a reduced-form type, as in (13). Given our earlier comments on observational equivalence, it is not clear from which structure these equations are derived. In the LBS model employment is disaggregated into four categories: (i) manufacturing, (ii) general government, (iii) primary and residual tertiary sectors, and (iv) self-employed and forces. The first is demand-determined, as in (2); (iii) is determined by an equation that can only be thought of as a reduced form, but also contains unemployment; (ii) and (iv) are assumed exogenous. Unemployment, as in (15), is the difference between the labour force and employment as determined in this way, with an equation estimated to explain the labour force. The LBS model is a good example of a model that is comprised of sectors rather than markets. Nominal wages are determined as a component of various factor incomes, rather than occurring in behavioural equations in the market for labour. Consequently three reduced forms are estimated for employment income generated in sectors (i)–(iii) above, of the form (13). This approach is even more striking when it is noted that often the *level* of earnings is not determined by such equations, only its rate of change.

The four sectors for employment in HMT are (i) manufacturing, (ii) other private, (iii) non-trading public, and (iv) North Sea. The first two are demand-determined, as in (2); (iv) is determined exogenously, while (iii) is calculated from the appropriate constant-price wage and salary bills. Total unemployment is the difference between labour supply (the labour force) and total employment. Registered unemployment is 80 per cent of this total. As noted above, the earnings equation is of the reduced form, (13).

CGP's labour market has only a set of disaggregated labour demand functions. Hence (2) forms the basis for 39 employment functions, disaggregated by industry, but contains two different features. First, Z^d is specified to contain hours of work, and so each labour demand equation is augmented by an hours-of-work equation, in spite of hours being treated exogenously in the former. Second, Z^d is specified to contain unemployment 'to test the hypothesis that the reactions involved are affected by the overall state of the labour market' (Peterson, 1982).

The last two models specify structural demand and supply equations. LPL's demand equation, (2), is unusual in that unemployment appears where employment should. The second equation can be interpreted in one of two ways – indeed, it is simultaneously called a 'supply/wage' equation. If again we replace employment by unemployment we have a standard supply equation, (1). Alternatively, one can recognize that underlying the estimated model is a notion of two labour markets, one competitive and one unionized. In the latter the wage is determined as a bargain, and a weighted average of this and the competitive wage yields a wage equation based upon market-clearing.

The CUBS labour market is a more elaborate version of the disequilibrium paradigm found in NIESR and CGP. It breaks employment into three components, whose total is demand-determined, as in (2). A labour supply schedule is estimated, as in (1), except that the dependent variable is the labour force, not employment. If the market clears, the difference between the two is the 'natural rate' of unemployment; otherwise there is a measure of 'involuntary' unemployment included. Then the real wage adjusts to its equilibrium growth rate as a function of involuntary unemployment, which is similar to (9). A separate wage adjustment equation specifies the equilibrium *level* of real wages as an arbitrary linear function of exogenous variables; arbitrary in that it does not correspond to the long-run solution of the model, as in (4), nor does this yield a unique value of the real wage when there is no involuntary unemployment. The natural rate of unemployment is solved out by specifying it as a linear function of real unemployment benefit and real supplementary benefit rates. The adjustment parameter in the wage equation indicates whether the model is market-clearing in spirit; this issue is examined in detail in Section 4.6.1.

In summary, all the models have an expression for labour demand, but only two have a supply equation (CUBS, LPL). The CUBS, LBS, NIESR, and HMT models have a wage equation. In only two cases is it possible to identify a market structure according to the framework outlined. In one of these (LPL) the model is market-clearing by construction, while in the other (CUBS) the presence of market-clearing depends on the particular parameter values used, an issue to which we return in Section 4.6. The LBS and HMT models have reduced-form relationships for employment and wages, and consequently it is not possible to specify the implied market mechanism. In the case of NIESR the wage adjustment equation includes unemployment, which would be consistent with market-clearing if all unemployment were voluntary. However, this rather begs the question, and whether the NIESR model is market-clearing or not also depends on how the target real wage is interpreted. Finally, the CGP model has only a labour demand schedule and hence no explicit labour market.

A comparative assessment of a complete market structure across all six models is thus not possible, and in the next three sections we examine the individual labour demand, labour supply, and wage relationships, which are, in any event, of interest in their own right.

4.3   Labour demand

4.3.1   Introduction

Each of the six models has at least one equation that can be classified as a labour demand equation, (2), repeated here for convenience:

$$n_t^d = -\alpha_1 W_t + \alpha_2 Z_t^d. \tag{2}$$

Most empirical models of labour demand, including those studied in this paper, derive their specification from the theory of the firm, whose behaviour is assumed to be representative of the degree of aggregation being modelled. Our concern is with the specification of Z_t^d, which may include lagged variables, and so a brief comment on dynamics is in order. The justification for the inclusion of n_{t-1} in Z_t^d is often *ad hoc*, although an argument based on quadratic adjustment costs has been provided by Tinsley (1971) and Sargent (1978) and is the basis of NIESR's version (see Wren-Lewis, 1982). Further lags can be included if the firm employs different types of worker characterized by different costs of adjustment (Nickell, 1981). In Sargent's analysis the firm's employment depends on an infinite forward vector of relative prices (and/or quantities); when an rth-order vector autoregression is used to forecast these expectations, the forward vector collapses to the current values plus $r - 1$ lags.

Apart from the dynamic specification, the actual menu of variables included in all but one of the equations under study (CUBS) arises from a very common approach to modelling labour demand. This specifies a production function whose arguments are labour, the capital stock, and time (as a proxy for techno-logical progress), and the so-called demand for labour is obtained by rearranging the marginal productivity condition for labour that arises in a profit-maximization problem. In an obvious notation we write the production function as

$$y = y(n, k, t) \tag{17}$$

and the marginal productivity condition for labour as

$$w/p = W = y_n(n, k, t). \tag{18}$$

Using (17) to eliminate k then yields

$$n^d = n^d(W, y, t), \qquad n_W^d < 0, n_y^d > 0. \tag{19}$$

A (log-)linear version of (19), with appropriate lags, is readily estimable. The general form (19) hides certain restrictions if the assumed technology is Cobb-Douglas, but if constant elasticity of substitution (CES) is assumed a general log-linear version of (19) is obtained, namely

$$\ln n = \left(\frac{1 + b/v}{1 + b}\right) \ln y - (1 + b)^{-1} \ln W, \tag{20}$$

where $(1 + b)^{-1}$ is the elasticity of substitution and v returns to scale (recall that as b tends to zero CES tends to Cobb–Douglas). One feature of (19) is the presence of output, which is an endogenous decision variable under profit maximization, and must be treated accordingly in estimation. Equation (19) is used in preference to (18) because it is often thought that the capital stock is badly measured and cannot be used as a regressor. Alternatively, it might be thought that output is given to the firm, and a cost-minimization framework is appropriate, but (19) should then include factor prices and not the price of output. Problems of measuring the user cost of capital then arise.

A common problem with the estimation of (19) is that the coefficient of the real wage is insignificant, so the variable is deleted. In order to justify a dynamic relationship between employment and output alone the work of Brechling (1965) and Ball and St Cyr (1966) may be cited. Here the production function (17) is inverted and 'desired' employment is postulated as a function of output and lags, capital being proxied by time. Using partial adjustment, the latent variable is substituted out, generating lags on employment. Under this interpretation it is important that the long-run coefficient on output be greater than unity, implying decreasing returns to scale. Our representation of this approach is

$$n^d = n^d(y, t), \qquad n^d_y > 1. \tag{21}$$

Alternatively, (21) can be thought of as a cost-minimizing labour demand schedule, dropping factor prices.

The papers by Hazeltine (1981) and Henry (1981) indicate the popularity of the class of models represented by both (21) and (19). Our discussion has emphasized profit maximization in a competitive environment, reflecting the traditional approach to modelling in this area. If, however, the firm faces a downward-sloping demand curve, (18) becomes $w/p = y_n(1 + \epsilon^{-1})$ and the price level is endogenous. If ϵ, the elasticity of demand for output, is constant, the problem is very similar to that described above.

In this framework the following questions seem pertinent:

(i)   Are the dynamic properties stable?
(ii) Are the long-run economic properties sensible?
(iii) Is output assumed to be an endogenous decision variable of the firm?
(iv) In a market for labour it might be argued that the real wage is endogenous: is it treated accordingly?
(v)   Are there any other variables included, and what is their economic rationale?

4.3.2   *LBS, LPL, NIESR, HMT, and CGP labour demand*

LBS's employment equation for manufacturing fits (19) neatly, provided we can interpret a 'competitiveness' term as the real wage. The competitiveness term can be written as

$$\ln \frac{w/(1.15p^w - 0.15q^w)}{y/n}$$

where p^w is the sterling price of world manufacturing exports and q^w is the price of wholesale manufacturing imports. Invoking a 'purchasing power parity' argument, one could replace $(1.15p^w - 0.15q^w)$ by the domestic price of manufactured goods, yielding a real-wage term. In addition, hours of work is added, presumably to capture some notion of substitutability between hours and men. The model may be written

$$(1 - 1.326L + 0.357L^2)n_t^d = (0.828 - 0.645L)h_{t-1} + (0.084 - 0.054L)y_{t-1}$$
$$- 0.014W_{t-2}$$

where L is the lag operator. The roots of the autoregressive polynomial are (0.950, 0.376). The response of labour demand to a permanent 1 per cent increase in each of the three forcing variables is shown in Table 4.1. It is clear

Table 4.1.   *Response of LBS labour demand (manufacturing) to a 1 per cent permanent increase in various forcing variables*[*]

	Hours	Output	Real wage
Long-run coefficient	5.90	0.97	−0.45
Percentage of long-run completed on impact	14.0	0.0	0.0
Median lag (quarters)	9.2	12.3	15.3
Mean lag (quarters)	16.2	18.9	21.7

[*] All variables in logarithms

that the response is very sluggish, which is due in part to the near unit root. This feature is quite common, particularly for manufacturing industry; see, for example, Muellbauer and Winter (1980) and Symons (1982). Notice that there is a near unit coefficient on output, but not on the real wage; consequently the long-run solution

$$n^d = 5.90h + 0.97y - 0.45W$$

could take on a CES interpretation with an elasticity of substitution of 0.45. However, the extremely large long-run coefficient on hours is a particularly poor feature of the model.

The LPL demand equation is of the form of (19) except that unemployment is used in place of employment. In order that we may compare with other models, we convert, using the implicit relationship $dn/dU = -0.137$, which ensures that long-run constant returns are imposed. This procedure is as in Minford (1983), and yields

$$n^d - y = -0.53W - 0.023t.$$

The equation has only one lagged dependent variable (recall that it is an annual model), whose coefficient is 0.53; thus the mean lag for a permanent 1 per cent change in either the real wage or output is 1.23 years. Just under half (47 per cent) of the adjustment is completed on impact.

The NIESR, HMT, and CGP labour demand schedules are of the form (21). In the NIESR model three of the four components of employment are demand-determined, assuming cost minimization, and the exact structure can be written as follows:

$$n_t = \alpha_1 n_{t-1} + \alpha_2 n_{t-2} + \beta_0 y_t + \beta_1 y_{t-1} + \beta_2 y_{t-2} + \gamma t. \tag{22}$$

The main features of the estimated equations are summarized in Table 4.2. As noted above, the economic content of this class of models is limited. Long-run constant returns for 'manufacturing' and 'other industries' has been tested and imposed; the increasing returns for 'mainly public' is an undesirable feature. In each sector the trend has a negative coefficient, which supports a technical progress rather than a capital stock interpretation. The adjustment to a permanent 1 per cent increase in output is sluggish, owing to one root being greater than 0.9.

Table 4.2 *Three employment functions in the NIESR model*

Dependent variable: $n_t^{\dagger}$

	Mfg	Other industries	Mainly public
Coefficients on			
n_{t-1}	1.665	1.129	0.745
n_{t-2}	−0.685	−0.203	0.157
y_t	0.114	0.227	0.0623
y_{t-1}	−0.036	−0.153	
y_{t-2}	−0.0575		
time	−0.00015	−0.00009	−0.00074
Roots of $\alpha(L)$	0.92	0.90	0.92
	0.74	0.22	−0.17
Mean lag (quarters)	7.0	7.7	10.8
Median lag (quarters)	3.2	3.8	6.8
95th percentile lag	25.5	26.8	33.3
Long-run coefficient	1.0*	1.0*	0.64
Percentage of long-run completed on impact	11.4	22.7	6.2

$\dagger$ n and y are logarithmic variables
* Imposed, i.e. parameterized so that $\alpha_1 + \alpha_2 + \beta_0 + \beta_1 + \beta_2 = 1$

In HMT, like NIESR, two separate components of employment are determined by (21), except that more lags on output are included and, more importantly, no lags on employment. In such a model,

$$n_t = \sum_{i=0}^{k} \delta_i y_{t-i} + \gamma t,$$

$\delta(L)$ may be interpreted as a finite approximation to the rational lag polynomial $\beta(L)/\alpha(L)$ in (22). In private non-manufacturing a tax term has been added picking up the effects of selective employment tax (SET) when in operation. The main features of the two equations are summarized in Table 4.3.

Table 4.3   *Two employment functions in the HMT model*
Dependent variable[*]: $n_t^\dagger$

	Private mfg	Private non-mfg
Coefficients on:		
y_t	0.122	0.116
y_{t-1}	0.143	0.135
y_{t-2}	0.130	0.134
y_{t-3}	0.107	0.106
y_{t-4}	0.089	0.059
y_{t-5}	0.079	0.020
y_{t-6}	0.073	0.030
y_{t-7}	0.058	–
time	−0.002	−0.0015
Mean lag (quarters)	2.9	2.0
Median lag (quarters)	2.1	1.4
Long-run coefficient[**]	0.80	0.60
Long-run coefficient on SET rate[***]		−1.847

[*] Adjusted for 'selective employment measures'
[**] Imposed, i.e. distributed lag coefficients are constrained to sum to the indicated value
[***] We write the term

$$\ln \frac{WFP + OCR + TXSET + YPNIR + NIS}{WFP + OCR + YPNIR + NIS} \quad \text{as} \quad \ln \left\{ \frac{W(1 + t_1)}{W} \right\}$$

where W is the wage bill including all taxes but SET. Note that this expression is approximately equal to t_1.

[†] n and y are logarithmic variables

The dynamic reactions of labour demand to a 1 per cent permanent increase in output are sensible. However, the imposed long-run elasticities of demand to output imply increasing returns to scale. The addition of the SET term in column (2) is noteworthy, as no other features of the opportunity cost of hiring labour are present and the semi-elasticity is enormous.

The basic structure of CGP's modelling of labour demand, like HMT and NIESR, is (21). However there are two different features: (i) actual hours per worker (including overtime) is added as an explanatory variable, which is then explained by an augmented hours equation; (ii) the aggregate unemployment rate is added. We can write this two-equation model as follows (see also Peterson, 1982):

$$n_t = \gamma_0 + \gamma_1 t + \gamma_2 U_t + \gamma_3 h_t + \gamma_4 h_{t-1} + \alpha_1 n_{t-1} + \beta_0 y_t + \beta_1 y_{t-1} \quad (23)$$

$$h_t = b_1 + b_2 t + b_3 U_t + b_4 h_t^n + b_5 h_{t-1} + b_6 h_{t-1}^n \quad (24)$$

where h^n refers to normal hours of work and h to actual hours of work. In (23) CGP test two hypotheses:

(i) $\alpha_1 - \gamma_3 - \gamma_4 = 1$, hours and men perfect substitutes in the long run;

(ii) $\alpha_1 + \beta_0 + \beta_1 = 1$, long-run constant returns to scale.

Two obvious sufficient conditions for (i) are the short-run restrictions

(iii) $\gamma_3 = -1; \gamma_4 = \alpha_1$

which are often imposed in estimation. Then (23) may be interpreted as a demand-for-man-hours equation, rather than a demand for men. When (iii) does not hold the demand-for-hours equation, (24), is of some importance but simply appears to capture a dynamic relationship between actual hours of work and normal hours of work (for a recent attempt at modelling hours, see Nickell, 1983). The inclusion of aggregate unemployment in a labour demand function is unusual, and is intended to reflect the impact of the state of the aggregate labour market on each industry's employment behaviour.

The treatment of the hours component of labour input varies across the other models. We restrict our comments to the following. NIESR estimate an hours equation for manufacturing; being derived from the same optimization problem as employment, it has much the same structure:

$$h_t = 0.78h_{t-1} + 0.25y_t - 0.18y_{t-1} - 0.06y_{t-3} + \text{dummies, constant, and trend}$$

where h_t is log average hours worked in manufacturing. Hours do not explain employment, but they do enter the wage adjustment equation. The LBS model has no hours equation, but lagged hours is a determinant of manufacturing employment. (It does not appear in the reduced form for primary and residual tertiary sectors.) Neither HMT nor CUBS model hours.

The labour demand equations for the five models can be summarized as follows. All the models contain output variables with constant returns to scale present in four out of five cases (HMT has increasing returns to scale). The HMT model has the quickest lag response, followed by that of Liverpool. In contrast, the response of employment to a change in output is more sluggish in the NIESR and LBS models. The LBS and LPL demand equations also contain real-wage terms, which are absent from the other models. Both have very similar long-run elasticities on this variable (of around one-half). This discussion has not dealt with the treatment of labour demand in the CUBS model; this is considered along with some more recent developments in the next section.

4.3.3   The demand for labour – more recent developments

The standard approach to modelling labour demand is summarized in equations (17)–(19). More recent empirical research (for example Symons, 1982; Andrews, 1983; Nickell and Andrews, 1983), together with the CUBS model, has included raw materials and energy, m, in the technology and used capital stock data to base a labour demand function on (18), suitably generalized. Given capital stock, the firm has two decision variables, and short-run profit maximization implies that the real price of raw materials, q/p say, is a determinant of labour demand. Generalizing (17), we write the production function as

$$y = y(n,m,k,t) \tag{25}$$

and the marginal productivity conditions as

$$w/p = W = y_n(n,m,k,t)$$
$$q/p = Q = y_m(n,m,k,t).$$

Solving these yields the labour demand function

$$n^d = n^d(W,Q,k,t) \qquad n^d_W < 0, \, n^d_Q \gtrless 0, \, n^d_k > 0 \tag{26}$$

in which only variables outside the firm's control are arguments. In this model, firms, unless they are demand-constrained, supply output and demand labour in response to relative prices, not quantities.

Equation (26) forms the basis of the CUBS labour demand schedule, with the further generalization that m is broken into its two constituent parts, namely energy, m_1, and raw materials, m_2, yielding

$$n^d = n^d(W, Q_1, Q_2, k, t).$$

This is estimated for private sector employment. In Table 4.4 we compare various features of the CUBS, Symons (1982), and Andrews (1983) models. The similarity between Andrews and CUBS results is striking, the only difference being a stronger real-wage effect in CUBS. The Symons model is slightly different, being more responsive to the independent variables. Whereas this may be due to the obvious differences, namely use of quarterly data, or a different sample, or the inclusion of the real rate of interest, a more likely explanation is simply that the manufacturing sector is more exposed, and a higher elasticity of demand for manufacturing output is reflected in more elastic labour demand via the Marshallian rules.

The long-run coefficients in the CUBS model are all correctly signed, as predicted by (26), noting that energy is a gross complement to labour, while raw materials are gross substitutes. The models differ in their adjustment paths to the long run. As indicated by the roots of the autoregressive operator, both Andrews and CUBS exhibit damped oscillations whereas Symons is monotonic. Figure 4.1 shows the dynamic response of the CUBS labour demand equation to a permanent 1 per cent fall in the real wage.

In the previous section it was concluded that all the employment demand equations possessed unit output elasticities except the HMT model. Here the lag response was most rapid, followed by that of LPL, with the response of NIESR and LBS more sluggish. The CUBS model of labour demand differs from the other models in that output does not enter the employment function; it also includes raw materials and energy as factors of production. Finally, its long-run real-wage elasticity is considerably larger than that of LBS and LPL — unity as against one-half.

Table 4.4   *Three alternative labour demand schedules*[*]

	(1)		(2)	(3)
n_{t-1}	1.50		1.13	1.06
n_{t-2}	-0.56		-0.50	-0.58
W_{t-1}	-0.053	W_t		-0.52
W_{t-5}	-0.406	W_{t-1}	-0.19	-0.13
Q_{t-1}	0.027	Q_{1t}	0.034	0.19
Q_{t-5}	0.051	Q_{2t}		0.08
I_t	0.0022	$Q_{1,t-1}$	-0.67	0.08
$\exp(2I_t)$	-0.000049	$Q_{2,t-1}$		-0.10
K_t			0.22	0.31
K_{t-1}	-0.15			
K_{t-2}	0.21			
t	0.000027			
Long-run solution				
W	-1.65		-0.51	-1.01
Q_1	-0.44		-0.088	-0.10
Q_2				-0.18
K	1.0[**]		0.59	0.61
Roots	0.8,0.7		$0.57 \pm 0.44i$	$0.53 \pm 0.54i$
Estimation	OLS		3SLS	3SLS
Sample	1961(1)–1977(2)		1950–79	1953–82

(1) Symons, manufacturing, quarterly
(2) Andrews, all employees in employment, annual
(3) CUBS, private sector, annual
[*] All variables except the real rate of interest, I_t, in logarithms
[**] tested and imposed

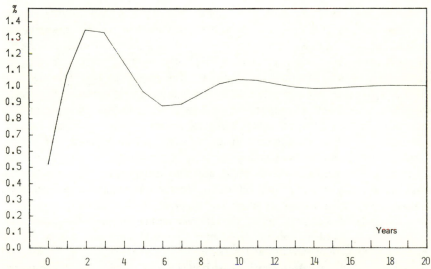

Fig. 4.1   Dynamic responses of CUBS labour demand to a permanent unit shock
in the real wage

4.4   Labour supply

4.4.1   Introduction

Most of the models considered in this study do not possess a labour supply function. In this section we consider the two that do, namely CUBS and LPL. Here we interpret the LPL model as including a supply equation, although Minford (1983) prefers to refer to the relationship as a wage bargaining model.

Labour supply equations typically have their basis in the utility-maximizing individual choice model, in which the consumer seeks an optimal allocation of time between work and leisure. The consumer is assumed to solve this (lifetime) problem intertemporally. In the general formulation of Sargent (1979), labour supply is derived as a function of the entire future sequences of real wages and one-period real interest rates. This analysis generalizes the work of Lucas and Rapping (1969), whose basic formulation restricts attention to the current real wage, W, an index of future real wages, W^*, and the current one-period real rate of interest, $R - \dot{p}^e$. Under weak conditions on the underlying preferences the Lucas–Rapping (henceforth LR) supply equation can be written

$$n_t^s = \delta_1 W_t - \delta_4 W_t^* + \delta_5 (R - \dot{p}^e)_t + \delta_2 Z_t^s. \tag{27}$$

This clearly generalizes (2), and serves as a reference point for our discussion. Key features are that the real interest rate has a positive influence on labour supply ($\delta_5 > 0$) and that a change in the real wage has a positive transitory effect ($\delta_1 > 0$) while the permanent response is inelastic ($\delta_1 - \delta_4 \approx 0$) or even backward-bending.

Equation (27) describes the labour supply decisions over time that result from the intertemporal allocation problem. This problem is posed at the individual level; hence each variable might also carry a second subscript, i, and Z_t^s might include not only the consumer's real wealth, via the intertemporal budget constraint, but also measures of personal characteristics and family circumstances. As in other areas of applied econometrics, two strands in the empirical literature can now be identified: the model as it stands might be estimated from cross-section data at the individual level, assuming that wages are exogenously determined at the market level; whereas aggregation over individuals yields a macroeconomic time series model, possibly dynamic in form. The labour supply area is unusual in the relative predominance of the former, which results from the availability of large micro-data sets. (An immediate contrast is with labour demand, where correspondingly rich data on individual firms are not available). While much of the detailed information obtained from cross-section studies has no counterpart in aggregate time series models, some cross-checking is possible, in particular concerning supply elasticities with respect to wages and the income replacement ratio. Moving from a cross-section framework to a time series model raises important aggregation issues. Some of these relate to the measurement of the independent variables in the equation, and in particular to the tax rate and income replacement ratio variables. Others are concerned with the dependent variable, where the cross-section evidence finds support for major differences between labour supply decisions for different groups. In particular, a common finding is that labour supply decisions are more responsive to economic factors for married women and part-time workers than for other sections of the labour force (see the survey by Greenhalgh and Mayhew, 1981). The labour supply relationships described in this section do not make any allowance for these aggregation points, although the disaggregated treatment of wage equations is examined in Section 4.5. Unfortunately, disaggregation is then by industry, which is an accident of the availability of the data, whereas cross-section studies suggest that disaggregation by skill and sex is more important.

An individual supply equation based on the theory described above has hours as the dependent variable; hence in an aggregate time series equation man-hours is the appropriate dependent variable, neglecting other problems discussed in the previous paragraph. In practice, either employment or the labour force is used. Of these, the former would seem more natural in a market-clearing context, given that the same variable should occur in both demand and supply. In a non-market-clearing model supply and demand are not necessarily equal, and using the labour force as the supply variable implies that unemployment is excess supply and hence involuntary. If (27) is to be modelled as it stands, then W^* and $(R - \dot{p}^e)_t$ are latent variables, and need treating appropriately, although the constructs that are used are seldom significant.

4.4.2 CUBS labour supply

The treatment of labour supply in the CUBS model corresponds to this framework. Z_t^s contains working population, a tax variable defined as 'threshold level of income tax expressed in terms of average earnings', and lags of the real wage and the dependent variable. Supply is modelled as the sum of employment and unemployment. Table 4.5 presents the estimated equation.

Table 4.5 *CUBS labour supply*

Dependent variable: n_t^s

Coefficients on[†]			Long-run
n_{t-1}^s	1.354		
n_{t-2}^s	−0.499		
W_t	0.060	W	0.262
W_{t-1}	−0.076		
W_{t-2}	0.054		
POP_t	0.830	POP	1.0[‡]
POP_{t-1}	−0.830		
POP_{t-2}	0.145		
$t_{2,t-2}^*$	0.034	t_2^*	0.237
Roots of autoregressive operator:	0.68 ±.20i		

[†] t_2^* is the tax variable defined in text
[‡] Imposed

The real-wage variable is appropriately defined as some measure of the real consumption wage; that is, it takes into account direct and indirect taxes. The long-run coefficient on the real wage is consistent with the small time series evidence available for the UK (see Andrews, 1983) and the evidence obtained from cross-section data. While the long-run is similar to that of LR, the short-run response is somewhat different. Consider an increase in the real wage. The interim multipliers, expressed as a proportion of the long-run, are 0.23 on impact, 0.25 after one year and 0.37, 0.52, 0.66, 0.79, 0.88, 0.94, 0.98, and 1.00 for subsequent years. Clearly, the response of labour supply is unusually slow — indeed, is more sluggish than labour demand.

4.4.3   LPL labour supply

The second equation of the LPL labour market is termed both 'supply' and 'wage', the former interpretation requiring a re-normalization. The estimated equation is

$$W_t = -0.034U_t + 0.012(RB + t_2)_t - 0.61POP_t + 0.72W_{t-1} + Z_t^s \quad (28)$$

where RB is the real benefit level, t_2 the income tax rate, and the vector Z_t^s includes in particular the unionization rate and the price inflation forecast error. The 'wage' interpretation is based on the following model (Minford, 1983). The labour market consists of two sectors, namely unionized and non-unionized. The competitive nature of the latter ensures that the real wage is determined by the intersection of supply and demand, but at a value only just above a floor given by the unemployment benefit level. The unionized real wage is determined by a mark-up on the competitive wage; the union sets the wage to maximize the income of its potential membership, given the firm's labour demand. A weighted average of the two real wages determines the observed real wage, which is estimated as in (28). The inclusion of unemployment and the exogenous labour supply variables comes about through a rearrangement of a labour supply equation that partially determines the competitive wage. However, Nickell (1984) argues that the degree of mark-up of the union's real wage depends on the position of the firm's demand schedule, and as the wage equation is the (observed) weighted average of both unionized and competitive wage, the influence of exogenous labour demand variables on the determination of the real wage should be included.

Because Z_t^d is not contained in (28), the alternative supply interpretation is admissible. Misgivings arise on dividing through by a coefficient not significantly different from zero; nevertheless, re-normalizing on U_t and using as before $dn/dU = -0.137$, the long-run labour supply equation is obtained as

$$n^s = 1.13W - 0.48(RB + t_2) + 2.45POP + Z^s.$$

Very little UK evidence is available on either unemployment or labour supply equations for comparison, although the responses appear relatively large in comparison with the CUBS model.

Having now examined both labour demand and labour supply relationships in the CUBS and LPL models, we observe that, while the long-run real wage elasticity in the labour demand model for CUBS is greater than the corresponding elasticity for LPL, the reverse situation holds for the labour supply equations, so that the sum of the absolute long-run elasticities is slightly greater for LPL than for CUBS (1.7 as against 1.3). However, a completely different picture emerges when we examine the sum of the impact elasticities, $\alpha_1 + \delta_1$, for each model: 4.3 for LPL and 0.6 for CUBS. This suggests that the patterns of adjustment differ between the two, reflecting the differing assumptions of wage adjustment in equating supply and demand. For these two models, where a clear model structure is set out, we consider the properties of the complete labour market in Section 4.6. Meanwhile in the next section we consider the wage relationships in the other models.

4.5 Wage equations

4.5.1 Introduction and general classification

This section discusses the determination of wages in the HMT, LBS, and NIESR models. The CUBS and LPL models each contain a more integrated treatment of the labour market and are discussed in Section 4.6. In contrast, the HMT, LBS, and NIESR labour sectors are either non-market-clearing or reduced-form relationships. The CGP model is also non-market-clearing, but in the standard version of the model wages are treated as predetermined and no further discussion is therefore relevant here. The wage sectors are first discussed in generic terms and are then compared in terms of various issues, expectations, pressure of demand effects, incomes policy, and so forth. A general summary of the wage sectors is given in Table 4.6.

In very general terms we can represent the wage adjustment equation, following the notation of Section 4.2, as

$$w_t - w_{t-1} = \lambda_1 y + \lambda_2 (p_t^e - p_{t-1}) + \lambda_3 Z_t^w + \lambda_4 \hat{W}_t + \lambda_5 W_{t-1} \qquad (29)$$

where w is the log of the nominal wage level, p the log of the price level, and y the pressure of demand for labour, which proxies excess demand, $n^d - n^s$. The augmented Phillips curve is a special case of (29) with $\lambda_4 = \lambda_5 = 0$.

The NIESR wage equation fits clearly into the real-wage resistance framework. It is described by Hall *et al.* (1983) as a bargaining model where wages are determined by pressure from the union side and where employers have the power to pass on wage increases through prices. The real wage target ($\hat{W}$) is set in gross terms, but the freely estimated equation gives an 'implausibly' high rate of growth of desired real wages, so this target growth rate is imposed at the historical average of $2\frac{1}{2}$ per cent per annum. The long-run solution to the wage equation is

$$W = -1.7u + 2.0h + \text{constant} + \text{trend}$$

where u is the unemployment rate and h is the level of hours.

Table 4.6   *Wage formation in the NIESR, LBS, and HMT models*

Model	Disaggregation	Determinants	Broad classification	Pressure-of-demand variable	Compensation for price change: (a) step; (b) continuing	Expectations	Incomes policy
NIESR	None	Real wage target, unemployment, prices, hours	Real-wage resistance	Unemployment rate	(a) Partial short-run Full long-run (b) Partial short- and long-run	Prices determined by AR(4) mechanism	None
LBS	3 sectors: Manufacturing	Consumer and producer prices; employer and employee taxes; competitiveness; output; interest rates; time	Reduced-form	Output	(a) Partial short-run Full long-run (b) as (a)	None	Dummy variables
	Public administration	Prices; earnings in manufacturing	?	None	(a) Partial short-run Full long-run (b) as (a)	None	Dummy variables
	Rest of private sector	Employment; female participation rate; retail sales; earnings in manufacturing	Reduced-form	Retail sales	(a) Partial short-run Full long-run (b) as (a)	None	None
HMT	3 sectors: Private	Output; consumer and producer prices; employee and employer taxes; public sector employment	Reduced-form	Output	(a) Partial short-run Full long-run (b) as (a)	None	None
	Central govt	Private sector earnings	Rule-of-thumb	None	—	None	None
	Local govt	Private sector earnings	Rule-of-thumb	None	—	None	None

The key equations in the wage sectors in the HMT and LBS models are reduced-form equations rather than real-wage resistance or augmented Phillips curve models. They therefore distinguish between employer and employee taxes and between producer and consumer prices. It is difficult to see how these equations are derived from the structure implied by the labour demand and supply mechanisms in the respective models. For example, in the LBS model terms such as employer tax rates and interest rates do not enter the reduced form for employment but appear in the wage adjustment equation. The presence of the real consumption wage and the real interest rate clearly derives from the Lucas–Rapping analysis described above and so corresponds to a supply-side effect. Of the two models, the Treasury wage sector has a stronger resemblance to the real-wage resistance paradigm than does the LBS model. The long-run solution to the Treasury equation is

$$w = \tfrac{1}{2}(p^c + p^y) + y - 0.5 \ln (1 - t_2) + 0.5 \ln (t_1) + 0.23n^g + \text{trend}$$

where p^c and p^y are the log of consumer and producer prices, respectively, t_1 is the employer tax rate, $1 - t_2$ is the retention ratio, and n^g the log of public sector employment. This may be rewritten as

$$W = y + \tfrac{1}{2}(t_1 + t_2 + t_3) + 0.23n^g + \text{trend}$$

where t_3 is the indirect tax rate and $W \equiv w - p$ where p is the pre-tax or producer price index. The long-run solution in the LBS model may be written in a similar fashion:

$$W = y - 0.12t_1 + 0.18(t_2 + t_3) + b_3R + \text{trend}$$

where R refers to the interest rate.

4.5.2   The specifications in detail

Disaggregation

Only the NIESR model deals with the determination of wages at the national level. Both the LBS and HMT distinguish the public from the private sectors and, in the former case, manufacturing from the rest of the private sector. In both models, however, public corporations are included in the private sector.

In the LBS model the determination of wages is driven mainly by the equation for earnings in manufacturing. Earnings in public administration diverge positively from manufacturing earnings if price inflation increases in the short term or if there is an incomes policy. In the long term there is a constant relativity between earnings in public administration and in manufacturing. Whereas earnings growth can differ between the public and manufacturing sectors only in the short run, the equation representing earnings in the non-manufacturing private sector of the economy has no similar implication. Here the long-run relativity depends on the level of demand in this sector and the price level. Both higher demand and a higher price level result in a higher wage relativity in this sector over manufacturing. Alternatively, the equation can be interpreted as showing that the *real* wage in this sector depends on demand and earnings in the manufacturing sector. The historical values of relative earnings in these sectors are shown in Figure 4.2.

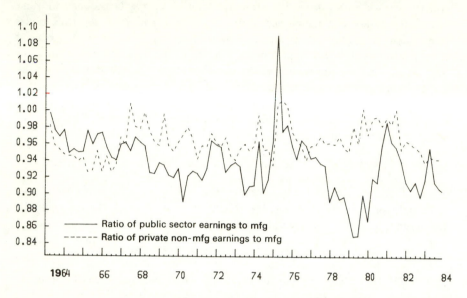

Fig. 4.2   Relative earnings data from the LBS model

In the HMT model public sector earnings are divided into two parts, namely central and local government, and in both of these sectors the growth of earnings follows that in the private sector with no lag. In allowing for a greater variation over the short term in the ratio of public sector to private sector wages, the LBS model appears to be supported by these data. Moreover, since the long-run manufacturing-rest-of-private-sector relativity need not be constant in the LBS model but the long-run manufacturing-public sector ratio is constant, the aggregate private sector-public sector ratio can vary in the long run, a feature at variance with the constancy of relative private sector-public sector earnings in the HMT model.

Recent empirical evidence (e.g. Capella and Ormerod, 1982; Foster *et al.*, 1984) suggests that earnings patterns differ between the private and public sectors. In particular, the evidence presented by Foster *et al.* suggests that it is important to include terms reflecting the evolution of earnings in other sectors as well as some of the standard determinants of earnings in each particular sector. The LBS framework comes closest to saying something about earnings interaction between sectors, hence the relevance of disaggregation on the determination of earnings at the national level. However, interaction terms are missing from the key equation, earnings in manufacturing, so that a recursive structure of wage settlements is implied. The HMT structure is also recursive, with the only feedback being from public sector *employment* to private sector wages.

The wage variable
Both the HMT and LBS models use earnings series for wages, but in the NIESR model the dependent variable is the wage rate (although the real-wage variable is defined in terms of earnings). Because of problems in obtaining useful measures of wage rates directly from the official data, the NIESR wage rate variable is a synthetic series. It is derived by dividing the effective level of average earnings (wages and salaries per employee) by an index of average hours worked.

Expectations
Of the three wage models considered here, only the NIESR model explicitly allows for expectations. In the other models expectations are implicitly assumed to be backward-looking. However, although expected prices enter the NIESR model, they are treated as weakly rational, using an autoregressive equation fitted to $p_t - p_{t-1}$; hence the NIESR wage model has in practice an extra-polative treatment of price inflation. Thus, in none of the models do genuine forward-looking variables enter. All shocks to the economy, whether known in advance or not, affect wages gradually through the fixed lag structure in each model.

Incomes policy
The three wage models under discussion either ignore incomes policy or treat it as a nuisance affecting the past behaviour of wages but with no potential role in the future. The estimated NIESR wage equation finds no significant effect for a dummy variable for the 1975–8 period, but it is not clear whether effects for other periods were tested. Work published by the NIESR (e.g. Henry *et al.*, 1976; Henry and Ormerod, 1978; Foster *et al.*, 1984) has consistently found significant policy effects.

The HMT model contains no policy terms, but since we do not know how much the equation is based on time series evidence and how much on *a priori* reasoning it is not possible to judge whether effects were tested for. The LBS model uses the dummy variable approach, finding three significant policy dummies for manufacturing and including two policy dummies for public sector earnings (of which only one is statistically significant) but none at all for earnings in the non-manufacturing private sector. The dummy variables in the public sector equation differ from those in the manufacturing equation but are not defined in the model manual.

The problems in attempting to allow for policy effects using the method-ology adopted by NIESR and LBS are many and to a large extent are rife in the applied economics literature. The principal problems (see Whitley, 1983, for a more detailed account) are the failure to incorporate any quantitative information about the policy (by adopting the dummy variable approach) and the assumption that incomes policy can be treated as an exogenous determinant of wages. In the original research on which the HMT wage equation is based, Wren-Lewis (1982) makes an attempt to remedy the first of these defects. Lawson (1981) and Whitley (1983) have also tackled the measurement problem. Work by Sargan (1980) and Desai *et al.* (1983) has attempted to allow for policy endogeneity. This point was forcefully made by Wallis (1971) over ten years ago, and most work in the area has been content to acknowledge the problem while proceeding to treat policy as exogenous.

Price effects

All three models contain price terms. In the NIESR model there is an adaptive mechanism on consumer prices. In the LBS and HMT models there are both level and difference terms in consumer and producer prices. Even though the coefficient of price expectations is less than unity in the NIESR model, the error correction mechanism inherent in the real-wage resistance hypothesis results in a long-run response of unity between prices and wages (see Figure 4.3). The

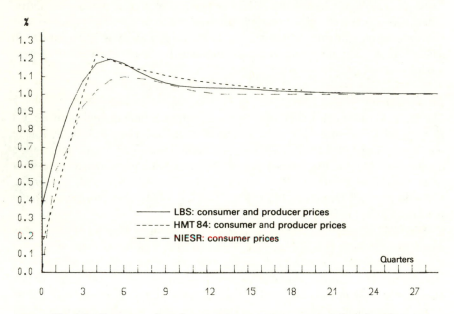

Fig. 4.3   Response of earnings to a permanent one per cent shock in prices

short-term overshooting in this response results from the lag structure assumed for real-wage adjustment together with the time series representation of expected prices. Real-wage adjustment starts only after three quarters, so that attempts to compensate for the initial reduction in real wages following a shock to prices comes on top of the adjustment of wages to prices. In other words, the real-wage adjustment does not allow for the fact that real wages may have been adjusting more recently. The rationale for such a lag on the real-wage term is not clear. If the shock is in terms of the rate of inflation, real wages move to compensate, with the long-run effect on real wages being equal to the level of the shock to price inflation. This lack of super-neutrality of real wages to the growth of prices in the NIESR model is due to a coefficient of less than unity on the term in expected inflation.

In both the LBS and HMT models, real wages are neutral with respect to both the price level and its rate of change. Both include consumer and producer prices. In the LBS wage system the equation for earnings in manufacturing gives a unit elasticity between producer prices and earnings but no long-run effect on earnings in the non-manufacturing private sector. For the system as a whole, the neutrality of real wages holds for an equal change in consumer and producer prices. There is more overshooting than in the NIESR case. The overshooting is also more pronounced in the HMT model, but all three models have quite similar speeds of adjustment.

It is not clear how much of the HMT wage system is based on empirical estimation and how much on *a priori* reasoning. Certainly, the neutrality of real wages is an important property which fundamentally affects certain overall model characteristics, as discussed below. Moreover, the division of the price response into consumer and producer prices also has important simulation properties. Because producer prices do not respond to changes in the rate of VAT, for example, the equation implies that wage compensation is asymmetrical between price changes arising from changes in indirect taxes and those arising from other cost changes. The definition of the price variables in the LBS model implies an asymmetry between changes in indirect taxes such as VAT and those such as specific duties. The latter has a larger impact on wages than a similar change in the rate of VAT. The institutional or empirical evidence on which such asymmetries are based appears to be somewhat lacking.

Pressure of demand

The pressure-of-demand variable in the NIESR model is a combination of terms in the level, first difference, and second difference of the unemployment rate. The long-run response is that a 1 percentage point increase in the level of unemployment lowers wages by $1\frac{3}{4}$ per cent. The dynamics of the response are also interesting and are shown in Figure 4.4. The unemployment change has no contemporaneous effect but then reduces earnings by 5 per cent in the next quarter, then has nil effect after two quarters before adopting a less jagged response. It is difficult to rationalize such a volatile short-run response, and no attempt is made in the description of the model by Hall *et al.* (1983). The 'natural' rate of unemployment implied by the equation is 12 per cent, although it is not clear that this is a meaningful estimate (see Thirlwall, 1983).

Compared with earlier estimates in the empirical literature, the pressure-of-demand effects in the three models appear quite large. Neither Henry and Ormerod (1978) nor Henry *et al.* (1976), among others, were able to find a

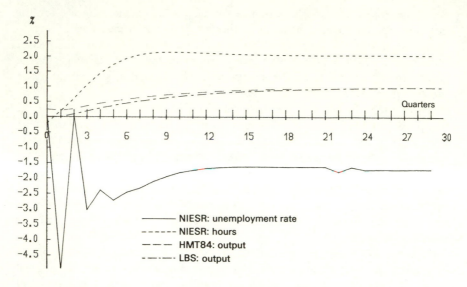

Fig. 4.4   Response of earnings to permanent one per cent shocks in the pressure of demand and hours

significant effect. However, Wadhwani (1982) and Wren-Lewis (1982) more recently found quite large pressure-of-demand effects.

The HMT and LBS models are of the reduced-form variety. The pressure-of-demand variable is therefore the level of output rather than the level of unemployment. In both models the long-run elasticity of wages with respect to the level of output is unity with the profile of adjustment shown in Figure 4.4. The basis for the HMT wage model is the work by Wren-Lewis (1982), who found much larger output elasticities, and the HMT wage equation has seen a reduction in this elasticity over time. The use of manufacturing output in the LBS manufacturing wage equation and the level of retail sales for the rest of the private sector, rather than the level of unemployment, has important implications. First, a rise in labour productivity in the overall model has no direct effect on earnings in either the LBS or HMT models; rather, any productivity response is obtained through its effects on labour costs and prices. However, it lowers earnings in the NIESR model through the impact on unemployment. Second, an increase in public sector expenditure in the LBS model has an impact on wages only if there are any effects on prices through the exchange rate, whereas in the HMT model a direct effect is embodied through the term in public sector employment.

Other variables

The NIESR wage model contains terms in the level and rate of change of hours worked in addition to the terms in prices and unemployment. There is a long-run elasticity between hours and wage rates of −3, and between hours and average earnings of -2 (see Table 4.7). The explanation of Hall *et al.* (1983) is that the hours terms allow for the cyclical influence of changing hours. Figure 4.4 shows the effect of reducing hours by one unit. The direction of the effect on earnings seems inconsistent with a cyclical influence; for one might then expect a fall in hours worked to be associated with lower overtime (and lower effective pressure of demand) and hence *lower* earnings. The dynamics of the hours terms allow for such an effect only in the very first period, after which the effect reverses sign and increases in magnitude. Rather, the equation appears to be capturing the long-term reduction in normal hours. The tendency has been for a reduction in normal hours to be compensated for by an increase in overtime working, so that there may be a positive influence on earnings.

Both the LBS and HMT models contain terms in employee and employer taxes. These can be justified in general as arising from the underlying demand and supply equations, although no such influences are present in the reduced-form explanations of employment. Both income and expenditure taxes paid by the employee (but not national insurance contributions) enter into the LBS tax variable, and it therefore differs from the corresponding variable in the HMT model, namely the retention ratio, which includes both income taxes and national insurance contributions (but not expenditure taxes). The long-run effect in the LBS model is that a 10 per cent increase in the rate of tax on the employee results in a 2 per cent increase in earnings, but the initial impact is perverse. A 10 per cent increase in the rate of employer tax reduces earnings in the long run by $1\frac{1}{4}$ per cent but there is a cyclical pattern in the adjustment to this long-run position (see Figure 4.5). In the HMT model both the retention ratio and the rate of employer tax have long-run elasticities of $\frac{1}{2}$ in absolute size so that equal changes in employee and employer tax rates leave earnings unchanged. Since in the LBS model employee taxes have a greater impact than employer taxes, an equal change in taxes increases wage inflation. Notice that NIESR include neither the retention ratio nor unemployment benefits, finding little econometric evidence for their presence. Indeed, none of the three models include a benefits variable in any of their wage equations, which contrasts with LPL as already noted.

In addition to the variables described above, the HMT model contains a term in public sector employment, the LBS manufacturing equation contains terms in international competitiveness and the real interest rate, while the equation for earnings in the rest of the private sector has terms in the change in employment and in the female participation rate. All three models contain a time trend.

The introduction of the level of public sector employment as a variable in the HMT model appears to be as part of the supply-side mechanism, but its role presupposes a constant labour force since one might theorize that an equal increase in labour supply and public sector employment will leave private sector earnings unchanged. The lag of two quarters on this variable appears arbitrary. The variable has important implications for policy simulations with the HMT model since it introduces a direct feedback from public expenditure to inflation.

Table 4.7　*Model responses of wages in the NIESR, LBS, and HMT models*
Effect on earnings of a 1 per cent permanent shock (%)

NIESR	Increase in price level	Increase in unemployment rate	Reduction in level of hours
Impact	–	–	-0.20
Period 2	0.57	-4.95	0.19
3	0.71	0.03	0.60
4	0.93	-3.02	1.05
8	1.09	-2.31	2.06
12	1.02	-1.73	2.12
16	1.00	-1.61	2.06
Long-run	1.00	-1.70	2.02

LBS	Increase in price level	Increase in output	Increase in competitiveness	Increase in taxes: Employer	Employee	Increase in Employment	Increase in female participation rate
Impact	0.10	0.13	-0.04	-0.05	-0.01	–	-0.49
Period 2	0.37	0.29	-0.09	-0.11	-0.02	–	-0.22
3	0.69	0.40	-0.11	-0.13	-0.01	-0.41	-0.10
4	0.92	0.52	-0.11	-0.12	0.01	-0.19	-0.05
8	1.18	0.76	-0.05	-0.10	0.07	0.07	0.04
12	1.05	0.94	-0.03	-0.11	0.12	–	-0.02
16	1.04	1.04	-0.02	-0.11	0.13	–	–
Long-run	1.00	1.00	–	-0.12	0.18	–	–

HMT	Increase in price level	Increase in output	Increase in taxes:		Increase in Public employment
			Employer	Employee	
Impact	0.15	0.24	−0.01	–	–
Period 2	0.43	0.21	−0.06	−0.03	–
3	0.72	0.26	−0.12	−0.08	0.03
4	1.00	0.36	−0.18	−0.12	0.06
8	1.15	0.64	−0.35	−0.27	0.13
12	1.08	0.80	−0.44	−0.37	0.17
16	1.05	0.88	−0.49	−0.42	0.19
Long-run	1.00	1.00	−0.50	−0.50	0.23

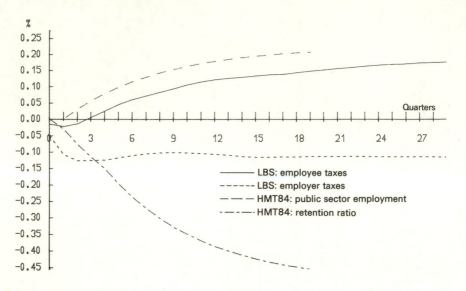

Fig. 4.5   Response of earnings to permanent one per cent shocks in taxes and public sector employment

Whereas the inclusion of public sector employment in the HMT model can be interpreted as a supply-side phenomenon, the role of a term in the change in international price competitiveness can be seen as a demand-side influence in the LBS model and can be interpreted as a real-wage influence (see Section 4.3). There is no long-run effect from a change in the level of competitiveness, but the short-run impact is to reduce earnings in manufacturing by just over 1 per cent for each 10 per cent change in the level of competitiveness. The interest rate term, however, reflects a supply-side effect. The actual variable used is the bank lending rate adjusted for inflation and lagged by two quarters. It can be rationalized as representing a wealth effect on labour supply, since as interest rates rise the value of private holdings of interest-bearing debt falls, implying a fall in net worth. The response of earnings is small. A 3 percentage point increase in the interest rate raises earnings by just under $\frac{1}{4}$ per cent in the long-run.

In the explanation of earnings in the non-manufacturing private sector, the change in employment in this sector (lagged by two quarters) and the change in the female participation rate have a negative influence. These both presumably reflect supply-side influences but have only a short-term effect on earnings. The employment effect peaks, not surprisingly, in the second period after the shock at a level of 0.4 per cent. The assumptions underlying this variable are similar to those behind the use of the public sector employment variable in the HMT model; that is, it is assumed that the increase in the level of employment occurs with a fixed supply of labour. In contrast, the inclusion of the female participation rate variable appears to be more plausible. The effects of increasing the level of the participation rate are only short-term and occur quite rapidly, with an effect of $\frac{1}{2}$ per cent on earnings from a 1 per cent increase in the participation rate within the same quarter.

Since all three models have a long-run elasticity of unity with respect to prices, the time trend included in the models can be interpreted as showing the equilibrium growth of real wages. All three models determine real wages within the labour market. The NIESR time trend represents the equilibrium growth of gross real wages, and a value of $2\frac{1}{2}$ per cent per annum is imposed, as noted above. In the LBS model the long-run growth rate of real wages is just under $1\frac{3}{4}$ per cent per annum, while the HMT time trend gives a value of less than 1 per cent per annum.

4.5.3 Implications of the wage models for the rest of the model

All the models have the property that there is no long-run relationship between the pressure of demand and the rate of inflation. They also imply that it is the real wage that depends on the level of excess demand and the other variables that appear in the equations. The long-run equilibrium growth of real wages depends on the value of the time trend in the models, for which the models all give different estimates. Because of the independence of the real wage from the price level, policies such as devaluation cannot work by changing the real wage. However, there is a time lag in response so that a temporary effect may emerge. In the NIESR model a continuously depreciating rate can be effective since real-wage adjustment is never completed.

The differentiation between producer and consumer prices also has important implications, as discussed above, while the use of public sector employment in the HMT private earnings equation introduces a direct inflation effect from higher public expenditure. The difference in the effects between a balanced increase in employer and employee taxes in the LBS and in the HMT models also has repercussions for simulations with the full model.

4.6 Analysis of two structural labour market models

4.6.1 The CUBS model

We now consider the first of the two models that represent the labour market in the structural form outlined in Section 4.2. Whether the CUBS model is market-clearing or not depends on particular parameter values, as already noted; the LPL model, market-clearing by construction, is considered subsequently. In each case the dynamic behaviour of the labour market sub-system is of especial interest.

To set the scene, consider a simple dynamic version of the model of Section 4.2. Let the supply equation contain the lagged real wage and the demand equation, lagged employment. Then equations (1) and (2) become

$$n_t^s = \delta_1 W_t + \delta_3 W_{t-1} + \delta_2 Z_t^s \tag{1'}$$

$$n_t^d = -\alpha_1 W_t + \alpha_3 n_{t-1} + \alpha_2 Z_t^d. \tag{2'}$$

Now assume that employment is always demand-determined, which implies that the real wage is never below the market-clearing real wage, and corresponding to $\Phi_t = 0$ in (14) we have

$$n_t = n_t^d.$$

Finally, suppose that partial adjustment describes the dynamic behaviour of the real wage when away from market-clearing, and that the market-clearing real wage has been substituted out, giving

$$W_t - W_{t-1} = \beta_4 (n^d - n^s)_t + \beta_3 Z_t^w. \tag{10'}$$

This corresponds to equation (10), with

$$\beta_4 = \beta_2 / (\alpha_1 + \delta_1)(1 - \beta_2).$$

We write (1'), (2') and (10') as follows:

$$
\begin{bmatrix} 1 & 0 & -\delta_1 \\ 0 & 1 & \alpha_1 \\ \beta_4 & -\beta_4 & 1 \end{bmatrix}
\begin{bmatrix} n_t^s \\ n_t^d \\ W_t \end{bmatrix}
=
\begin{bmatrix} 0 & 0 & \delta_3 \\ 0 & \alpha_3 & 0 \\ 0 & 0 & 1 \end{bmatrix}
\begin{bmatrix} n_{t-1}^s \\ n_{t-1}^d \\ W_{t-1} \end{bmatrix}
+
\begin{bmatrix} \delta_2 Z_t^s \\ \alpha_2 Z_t^d \\ \beta_3 Z_t^w \end{bmatrix}
$$

or, in an abbreviated notation,

$$B_0 y_t = B_1 y_{t-1} + Z_t. \tag{30}$$

This system has a unique long-run solution provided that $(B_0 - B_1)$ is non-singular, and has a stable adjustment path provided that the roots of the characteristic equation $|B_0 z - B_1| = 0$ lie inside the unit circle. Particular interest centres on the coefficient β_4, for neither condition is satisfied if $\beta_4 = 0$. In this case there is no feedback from labour market conditions to the real wage, and equation (10') reduces to

$$W_t = W_{t-1} + \beta_3 Z_t^w$$

indicating that the real wage changes only in response to institutional or other exogenous factors.

Consider now the equations of the CUBS model that correspond to (1'), (2'), and (10'), but with more general dynamics. Neglecting most of the variables that are exogenous to this sub-system, the equations are:

$$(1 - 1.353L + 0.499L^2) \ln n_t^s = (0.058 - 0.076L + 0.054L^2) \ln W_t + \ldots \tag{31}$$

$$(1 - 1.061L + 0.578L^2) \ln n_t^d = -0.521 \ln W_t + 0.313 k_t + \ldots \tag{32}$$

$$(1 - L)\ln W_t = -0.207(1 - L)\ln W_{t-2} - 0.017(\ln U_t - \ln n_t^s) + \ldots \tag{33}$$

The capital stock variable k_t is chosen to be the forcing variable in our dynamic analysis. The labour market model is completed using the standard identity defining unemployment,

$$U_t = n_t^s - n_t^d \qquad (34)$$

where U is measured in persons. In equation (33) the term in $(\ln U_t - \ln n_t^s)$, the logarithm of the unemployment rate, proxies the theoretical construct $(n^d - n^s)_t$.

The model is almost log-linear, the unemployment identity being the exception. Substituting (34) into (33) yields

$$(1 - L)\ln W_t = -0.207(1 - L)\ln W_{t-2} - 0.017 \{\ln(n_t^s - n_t^d) - \ln n_t^s\} + \ldots \quad (35)$$

indicating that the departure from log-linearity is confined to a single term. This makes it possible to obtain a local approximation to a log-linear system, to which conventional methods of dynamic analysis can be applied. The model of equations (31), (32), and (35) can be represented in the form of the simple dynamic model (30) on extending this in three ways. First, the endogenous variable vector y_t is defined in terms of the logarithms of n_t^s, n_t^d, and W_t. Second, additional lags are necessary given the more general dynamics of the CUBS model. Third, totally differentiating the system then gives the representation (d denotes total differential)

$$B_{0,t}dy_t = B_1 dy_{t-1} + B_2 dy_{t-2} + B_3 dy_{t-3} + dZ_t \qquad (36)$$

where the leading coefficient matrix is

$$B_{0,t} = \begin{bmatrix} 1 & 0 & -0.058 \\ 0 & 1 & 0.521 \\ \dfrac{0.017\, n_t^d}{n_t^s - n_t^d} & \dfrac{-0.017\, n_t^d}{n_t^s - n_t^d} & 1 \end{bmatrix}.$$

The nonlinearity is reflected in the dependence of this coefficient matrix on $n_t^d / (n_t^s - n_t^d)$, a measure closely related to the inverse of the unemployment rate; but for given values of these variables methods of linear analysis can be applied to calculate adjustment paths, multipliers, and so forth that are valid in that neighbourhood. Of course, this is only an approximation, because the values of n_t^d and n_t^s should change continuously in response to an initial shock, thereby making the coefficient matrix non-constant. The question of how nonlinear the model is rests on how $n_t^d / (n_t^s - n_t^d)$ changes, and this can be considered in a second experiment, namely a dynamic simulation of the actual labour market model by standard numerical methods. Both of these exercises are carried out side by side. The model is assumed to be in static equilibrium in 1984, and therefore in the linear experiment 1984 values for n^s and n^d are substituted in to the coefficient matrix $B_{0,t}$. In the nonlinear experiment the model is solved forwards under the set of exogenous assumptions provided in the CUBS forecast (but with zero residual adjustments), blocking out the rest of the model, to yield

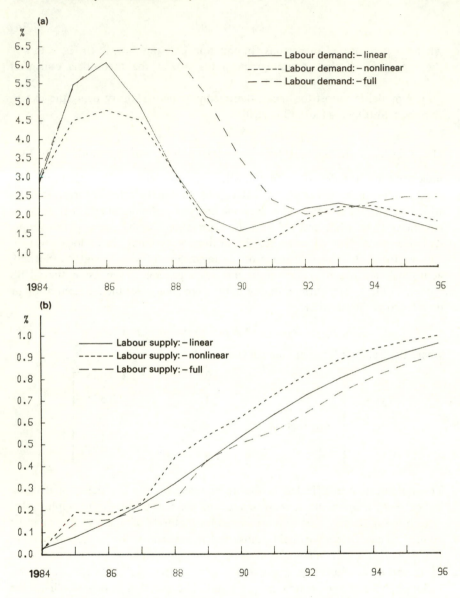

a base run. A 10 per cent permanent increase in the capital stock is then imparted in 1984 and the model is solved again, the differences between the new
solution and the base run giving the analogues of the dynamic multipliers in the
linear experiment. Finally, a full model simulation is reported in which the
labour market is allowed to interact with the rest of the model. A shock is
imparted to labour demand, via its residual, that induces an endogenous change
in the capital stock of 10 per cent. All three experiments are reported in Table
4.8, and shown in graph form in Figure 4.6.

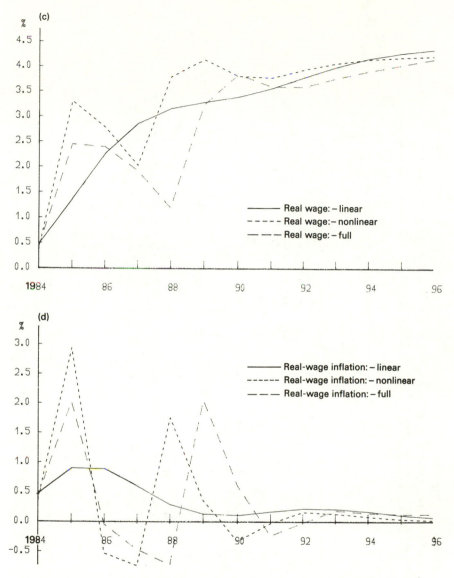

Fig. 4.6   Response of the CUBS labour market to a ten per cent shock in the capital stock

The simulation of the labour market sub-block reveals that the response paths for both the real wage and labour demand are characterized by two large cycles before settling down close to their long-run levels, which, however, are not achieved within the simulation period. Taking the long-run increase in labour demand to be approximately 1.5 per cent, labour demand responds on impact by jumping to twice its long-run level, peaks at three times this value, and completes the first cycle after about eight years. This unusual response path

Table 4.8   *Response of the CUBS labour market to a shock in the capital stock*

Percentage total changes over time for (i) linear approximation; (ii) simulation of labour market sub-block; (iii) full dynamic simulation, in response to a permanent increase in the capital stock of 10 per cent

	(1)	(2)	(3)	(4)	(5)	(6)	(7)	(8)	(9)	(10)	(11)	(12)	(13)† $\left(\dfrac{n^d}{n^s - n^d}\right)_t$	(14)† $\dfrac{100(n^s - n^d)_t}{n_t^d}$
	$\ln n_t^d$			$\ln n_t^s$			$\ln W_t$			$D \ln W_t$				
	(i)	(ii)	(iii)	(i)	(ii)	(iii)	(i)	(ii)	(iii)*	(i)	(ii)	(iii)*		
1984	2.88	2.93	3.02	0.028	0.022	0.024	0.48	0.37	0.42	0.48	0.37	0.42	9.93	10.07
1985	5.47	4.51	5.38	0.081	0.192	0.142	1.37	3.30	2.44	0.90	2.93	2.02	27.15	3.68
1986	6.08	4.78	6.38	0.149	0.181	0.157	2.27	2.78	2.39	0.89	−0.53	−0.05	129.64	0.77
1987	4.93	4.53	6.44	0.229	0.234	0.202	2.86	2.03	1.92	0.60	−0.74	−0.47	107.44	0.93
1988	3.20	3.20	6.39	0.324	0.440	0.247	3.16	3.79	1.19	0.29	1.75	−0.73	34.01	2.94
1989	1.96	1.75	5.20	0.429	0.542	0.433	3.29	4.14	3.24	0.13	0.36	2.05	16.94	5.90
1990	1.58	1.14	3.52	0.537	0.625	0.505	3.40	3.81	3.84	0.11	−0.33	0.61	12.65	7.90
1991	1.82	1.36	2.38	0.638	0.727	0.558	3.57	3.78	3.60	0.17	−0.03	−0.24	11.60	8.62
1992	2.16	1.86	2.00	0.728	0.820	0.645	3.79	3.94	3.59	0.22	0.16	−0.02	11.63	8.60
1993	2.29	2.19	2.08	0.803	0.887	0.734	4.00	4.07	3.77	0.21	0.13	0.18	11.64	8.59
1994	2.13	2.22	2.30	0.866	0.935	0.806	4.17	4.15	3.91	0.17	0.08	0.14	11.04	9.06
1995	1.84	2.03	2.44	0.919	0.971	0.864	4.28	4.19	4.03	0.11	0.04	0.12	10.38	9.64
1996	1.58	1.80	2.44	0.963	0.997	0.912	4.35	4.21	4.15	0.069	0.02	0.12	9.94	10.06
1997	1.45			1.000			4.40			0.052				
1998	1.43			1.032			4.45			0.053				
1999	1.46			1.058			4.51			0.056				
2000	1.47			1.079			4.56			0.055				
2001	1.44			1.096			4.61			0.046				
2002	1.39			1.110			4.64			0.035				
2003	1.33			1.122			4.67			0.026				
Long-run	1.19			1.19			4.82			0.000				

* Real wage to employees

† Correction factor $n_t^d/(n^s - n^d)_t$ for 1984 is 9.929, which corresponds to an unemployment rate, $(n^s - n^d)_t/n_t^s$, of 9.15 per cent. Column (13) displays the correction factor over the forecast period; column (14) its inverse.

reflects the demand equation dynamic properties described in Section 4.3. The cyclical pattern of the real wage is similar, and indicates that most of the action in the labour market is on the demand side. Labour supply grows at approximately 0.075 per cent per year, and so unemployment (not shown) mirrors labour demand. One further indication of the sluggishness of the labour market is provided by the rate of change of the real wage, which settles down close to its long-run value of zero after eight years.

This dynamic behaviour can be explained by the linear approximation (36). For supply and demand the approximation reproduces the full simulation quite accurately, but it does not capture the cyclical nature of the real wage. This is not surprising, as there is a large collapse in unemployment in 1986–7 in the base run, and the variation in unemployment (column 13, Table 4.8) reflects the varying degree of accuracy available in the approximation. With the 1984 values of n_t^s and n_t^d we obtain

$$\det (B_{0,t} - B_1 - B_2 - B_3) = 0.0157$$

and the roots of the characteristic equation as

$$0.85, \ 0.50 \pm 0.58i, \ -0.00 \pm 0.46i, \ 0.69 \pm 0.20i.$$

A comparison with (30) is revealing. Since the correction factor $n_t^d / (n_t^s - n_t^d)$ has the value 9.929 in 1984, the coefficient in $B_{0,t}$ that corresponds to β_4 in (30) is 0.17, and for this reason it is not surprising to find that the characteristic equation has one large root (0.85). Consequently we conclude that the sluggish behaviour is a result of the very small coefficient on the excess supply term in wage adjustment, equation (33). If underlying this equation is the partial adjustment equation (10), we may extract the adjustment parameter β_2 from the relation

$$\beta_4 = 0.167 = \beta_2 / (\alpha_1 + \delta_1)(1 - \beta_2)$$

given contemporaneous real-wage elasticities in supply and demand of $\alpha_1 = 0.52$ and $\delta_1 = 0.08$, yielding $\beta_2 = 0.091$. This very small reaction is the cause of the sluggish dynamic response of the CUBS labour market.

We now consider the dynamic interrelationship of labour supply, labour demand, unemployment, and real wages following a shock to labour demand. The impact response is illustrated in Figure 4.7. The initial equilibrium (n_0^d, n_0^s, W_0) is represented by the points A_0 and B_0, and the initial equilibrium value for unemployment, U_0, by the distance between the two points. The response to the demand shock is illustrated by a rightwards shift in the demand schedule and an increase in the real wage. The new values for the four endogenous variables are represented by A_1 and B_1. Given the more elastic nature of labour demand relative to labour supply, we observe a larger increase in the former. The real wage also increases. The ensuing dynamic response of the system is dominated by the wage adjustment equation, which indicates that the long-run level of real wages is higher than the impact value. It is possible to identify two

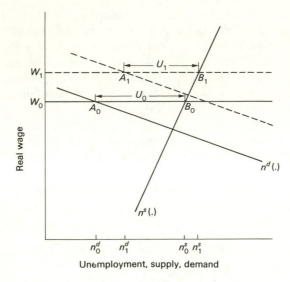

Fig. 4.7   Labour demand and supply interrelations

separate influences on labour demand from one period to the next. The first is a negative influence, of demand responding to the increase in real wages, period by period. The second is the dynamic response of demand to the original shock which was illustrated in Figure 4.6. The time taken for the whole system to approach the long run is determined by the size of the response of real wages to excess supply, as indicated in the earlier analysis.

Finally, we note the reaction of the labour market when allowed to interact with the rest of the model. Reference to Figure 4.6 and Table 4.8 indicates that the sluggish response of the labour market is not ameliorated when aggregate demand is taken into account − indeed, the length of the first cycle is increased by two years.

4.6.2   The LPL model

In this section we consider the dynamic interrelationships implied by the two equations previously discussed, namely the demand and 'supply/wage' equations. To focus on these questions we neglect most of the variables that are exogenous to this sub-system, and write the (log-linear) equations as

$$
\begin{bmatrix} 1 & -1.82 \\ 0.034 & 1 \end{bmatrix}
\begin{bmatrix} U_t \\ W_t \end{bmatrix}
=
\begin{bmatrix} 0.53 & 0 \\ 0 & 0.72 \end{bmatrix}
\begin{bmatrix} U_{t-1} \\ W_{t-1} \end{bmatrix}
+
\begin{bmatrix} -3.44 y_t \\ 0.12(RB + t_2)_t \end{bmatrix}.
\tag{37}
$$

The forcing variable for the purpose of our dynamic analysis is chosen to be real benefits, since considerable interest has centred on the magnitude and nature of the responses to changes in this variable and the replacement ratio. The long-run partial elasticity of unemployment with respect to real benefits implied by the second equation is 3.5. The implicit constancy of the real wage in this calculation may be relaxed first by considering the labour system on its own, using standard linear techniques, and second by allowing the rest of the model to interact with the labour market, through a full simulation.

To consider the long-run elasticities with respect to the real benefits in the face of the joint determination of unemployment and wages, we solve the equations

$$
\begin{bmatrix} 0.47 & -1.82 \\ 0.034 & 0.28 \end{bmatrix} \begin{bmatrix} dU/dRB \\ dW/dRB \end{bmatrix} = \begin{bmatrix} 0 \\ 0.12 \end{bmatrix}
\tag{38}
$$

to obtain an unemployment elasticity of 1.13, which is considerably lower than 3.5. Moreover, given lagged dependent variables in each equation, dynamic adjustment to these long-run values is somewhat sluggish. The reduced form of this system is

$$
\begin{bmatrix} U_t \\ W_t \end{bmatrix} = \begin{bmatrix} 0.50 & 1.23 \\ -0.017 & 0.68 \end{bmatrix} \begin{bmatrix} U_{t-1} \\ W_{t-1} \end{bmatrix} + \begin{bmatrix} 0.21 & -3.24 \\ 0.11 & 0.11 \end{bmatrix} \begin{bmatrix} RB_t \\ y_t \end{bmatrix}
\tag{39}
$$

and the roots of the autoregression are $(0.59 \pm 0.11i)$. The cumulative multipliers for both U_t and W_t are given in Table 4.9. Since the roots are a complex conjugate pair oscillatory behaviour is implied, but the real part dominates, and there are only small oscillations following the first passage through the long-run position. In the case of unemployment this occurs after 14 years.

It is potentially misleading to consider this issue only within the labour

Table 4.9 *Response of the LPL labour market to a change in real benefits*

Dynamic multipliers (cols (2) and (4)) and percentage of long run completed (cols (3) and (5)) after n years in response to a permanent change in real benefits

n (1)	Unemployment		Real wage	
	(2)	(3)	(4)	(5)
		%		%
0	0.206	18.2	0.113	38.8
1	0.448	39.7	0.186	63.8
2	0.659	58.4	0.231	79.5
3	0.820	72.7	0.258	88.8
4	0.935	82.8	0.275	94.2
5	1.011	90.0	0.283	97.2
6	1.060	93.9	0.288	98.8
7	1.090	96.6	0.290	99.6
9			0.292	100.0
14	1.129	100.0		

market, and we now consider the effect on unemployment when aggregate demand is taken into consideration. A cut in real benefits lowers real wages and increases labour demand, which is consistent with the higher output supply. This increase in supply is taken up either in increased sales (output) or in lower prices, depending on the structure of aggregate demand. It is important to note that this is the only endogenous channel by which the rest of model can influence the subsystem (38). In Table 4.10 we report the results of a complete model simulation given a 10 per cent cut in real benefits. First, output is treated as an exogenous variable, the comparison with Table 4.9 providing a check on our calculations: it is seen that these agree to an acceptable degree of accuracy. Then, output is treated as an endogenous variable, and the complete model simulation exercise is repeated.

Table 4.10 *Simulations of the LPL labour market in response to a 10 per cent cut in real benefits*

Years	Unemployment $(1)^*$	$(2)^{\dagger}$	Output $(3)^{\dagger}$	Real wage $(4)^*$	$(5)^{\dagger}$
0	−0.205	−0.690	0.151	−0.113	−0.097
1	−0.447	−1.124	0.177	−0.186	−0.147
2	−0.661	−1.599	0.183	−0.231	−0.172
3	−0.823	−1.845	0.188	−0.259	−0.179
4	−0.934	−1.979	0.194	−0.275	−0.182
5	−1.010	−2.048	0.195	−0.283	−0.181
6	−1.061	−2.067	0.194	−0.288	−0.181
7	−1.094	−2.078	0.191	−0.290	−0.180
8	−1.109	−2.086	0.191	−0.291	−0.179
9	−1.115	−2.072	0.186	−0.292	−0.178
10	−1.123	−2.053	0.184	−0.292	−0.179
11	−1.127	−2.048	0.185	−0.292	−0.179
12	−1.127	−2.046	0.183	−0.292	−0.179
13	−1.127	−2.046	0.186	−0.292	−0.179

* output exogenous
† output endogenous

Comparing columns (1) and (2), we see that, when the influence of output on labour demand is taken into account, the effect of real benefits on unemployment is 3.4 times larger on impact, and 1.8 times larger in the long run. Column (3) indicates the response of output to the cut in real benefits, which is not particularly large. The difference, therefore, is due mainly to the large output-unemployment elasticity. This depends on two structural effects, namely the real-wage effect in the (labour) supply/wage equation, and the implicit relationship between employment and unemployment. The partial elasticity of unemployment with respect to the real wage in the wage/supply equation is 8.2, which translates into an elasticity on labour supply of 1.13. As already noted, this is uncharacteristically large, and depends on an imputed value of −0.137 for $d \log (\text{employment})/d \log (\text{unemployment})$, which might be questioned in the absence of any econometric evidence for such a relationship.

In summary, the long-run elasticity of unemployment with respect to real benefits is estimated as 3.5 in the supply/wage equation, falls to 1.13 when labour market interactions are allowed for, and rises to 2.05 when the relationships between the labour market and the rest of the economy are taken into account. This exercise illustrates the general danger of basing labour market policy analysis on just one of the equations considered in previous sections, whether these be demand, supply, or wage equations.

4.7 Summary and conclusions

One of the intentions of this study was to see which market paradigm was appropriate to the labour market sectors of the six macroeconomic models. In practice, only two of the models can be classified by their structure. In the others the underlying market is not defined either because there are insufficient relationships (e.g., CGP, where there is only a labour demand equation) or because the relationships are reduced forms. The CUBS and LPL models do however have a clear structure, and while that of Liverpool is market-clearing by construction, the CUBS model is more general and depends on the precise values of some parameters. It turns out, however, that in practice the CUBS model is non-market-clearing because the wage adjustment equation delivers a large root to the labour market sub-system. This ensures that the real wage exhibits very sluggish adjustment towards its market-clearing level.

The modelling of labour demand can be summarized as follows. In the NIESR, CGP, and HMT demand equations output is the main explanatory variable. In the first two cases there is a unit elasticity of employment with respect to output and in the HMT equations the elasticity is less than unity. The CGP and LBS models include an hours-of-work dimension to the labour input, but this represents more of an *ad hoc* attempt to capture some simple dynamic relationship between hours of work and normal hours than an exploration of the interrelationship between men, hours, and output. The NIESR model contains a separate equation for hours, but this is basically a short-run adjustment relationship to output. Time trends play a significant role in all these demand equations, one interpretation of which might be that the remainder of the equation represents a model of the cyclical path of employment with little, if anything, to say about longer-term developments in labour demand. In contrast, the LBS and CUBS models do not contain time trends.

The LBS and LPL demand equations also have unit elasticities and real-wage elasticities of just under one-half. The main difference between the two is that full adjustment takes place within the time period for LPL (one year), while adjustment is very sluggish in the LBS model, with a mean lag of between four and five years. The CUBS model reflects some of the more recent developments in labour demand and treats output as a decision variable which is then omitted from the demand equation, where raw materials and energy are distinguished as factors of production. The real-wage elasticity is unity but the adjustment path is oscillatory.

Labour supply functions can be summarized more succinctly in that they appear in only two of the models. Here the real-wage elasticity in the LPL model is much larger than for the CUBS model, in contrast to the demand function results. As with the labour demand functions, the hours dimension of labour supply is ignored. Although there is a substantial body of empirical evidence relating to labour supply using cross-section data, there are very few relevant time series labour supply equations. This may well be a cause of the lack of labour supply relationships in macroeconomic models.

Developments in wage equations have led to the virtual demise of the Phillips curve as the standard wage relationship in macromodels. The NIESR model uses a real-wage resistance model, while the LBS and HMT models use a more *ad hoc* reduced-form relationship. All three models exhibit homogeneity, but whereas the LBS and HMT show homogeneity in terms of both levels and first differences, the NIESR possesses homogeneity only in terms of levels. HMT and LBS have some disaggregation, but this is more of a recursive nature and does not reveal any of the potential interrelationships between wages in different sectors. While the NIESR model contains the traditional unemployment variable in its wage equation, the LBS and NIESR models have output as the pressure-of-demand variable. Both have an output elasticity of unity, and the NIESR unemployment effect is quite large by recent empirical standards. The use of output rather than unemployment has interesting implications for the full model since an increase in productivity growth will (for given output) operate indirectly through prices in the LBS and HMT models whereas there is a direct effect through unemployment in the NIESR model. One instance in which wage equations have not developed much is in their treatment of incomes policy. The treatment still tends to be that of the dummy-variable approach, ignoring endogeneity problems, and therefore the models can say nothing of very much use about incomes policy, either past or future. Perhaps the recent work of Lawson (1981) (not included in the forecasting version of the CGP model) and Desai *et al*. (1983), among others, might stimulate some new interest in this question.

Chapter 5

The Assessment of Monetary and Fiscal Policy

5.1 Introduction

This chapter is concerned with general issues of monetary and fiscal policy as dealt with by five UK models. Our central purpose is to examine how far these models are appropriate for answering some common questions about fiscal and monetary policy and to contrast how different models might be more relevant for certain issues than others. It is not the role of this chapter to examine critically how the models address the important theoretical issues in demand management. Nor do we describe the transmission mechanisms of fiscal and monetary policy in the models; evidence relevant to this is presented in Chapter 2.

In order to undertake this analysis of the models we first raise some of the general questions involved in measuring fiscal and monetary stance. This is done in Section 5.2. The observation that measures of monetary and fiscal stance are not model-free naturally leads to descriptions of the formal use of models in measuring policy influence in Section 5.3. In Section 5.4 we then examine the interrelationship between monetary and fiscal policy in the models and in Section 5.5 we discuss the usefulness of the various models in policy exercises. The final section contains summary and conclusions.

5.2 General issues in measuring monetary and fiscal stance

The basic problem in measuring or defining policy stance is that there is more than one policy instrument. For example, in the fiscal policy area there is a whole set of tax rates and expenditure items. The issue is simply how to combine all the potential instruments in order to make a statement about fiscal policy stance. Economic commentators often refer to the 'tightness' or otherwise of policy, so they are at least making some implicit judgement about the relative weighting of policy instruments. Summary indicators are also useful in considering the relative efficacy of fiscal and monetary policy. In the discussion that follows issues concerning the measurement of fiscal policy stance receive more attention, principally because this reflects the existing literature, although this may be a result of more fundamental problems in defining monetary policy stance.

The simplest way of combining tax and expenditure effects is to look at the actual budget deficit, which we refer to as the public sector financial deficit (PSFD); this differs from the more common public sector borrowing requirement in respect of certain financial transactions. All the models under consideration produce an estimate of the public sector deficit although the LPL model differs in giving the measure in constant-price form.

Further measures are discussed extensively by Blinder and Solow (1974), and a condensed version is provided by Artis and Green (1982). These issues traditionally focus on the short-run Keynesian fix-price *IS/LM* model, which we may write as follows:

$$y = c(y - T, r) + g \qquad 0 < \frac{\partial c}{\partial(y - T)} \equiv c' < 1, c_r < 0$$

$$T = T(y, t) \qquad\qquad T_y > 0 \; T_t > 0 \tag{1}$$

$$m = l(r, y) \qquad\qquad l_r < 0 \; l_y > 0$$

where

y is (real) income
c is (real) private consumption and investment expenditure
g is (real) government expenditure
T is (real) income tax revenues
r is nominal rate of interest
m is (real) quantity of money
t is the income tax rate
and subscripts denote partial derivatives.

The change in the budget surplus can be expressed as

$$dT - dg = T_y dy + T_t dt - dg.$$

Common criticisms of the actual budget surplus as a measure of fiscal stance are as follows. The first, as stressed by Blinder and Solow, arises from the balanced budget theorem, which states that an increase in government expenditure balanced by an increase in tax revenue (by increasing t) increases the level of income. If income is the only variable of interest, it follows that it can be kept constant by running deficits. The second is that it fails to distinguish between discretionary and automatic effects on the budget surplus because of its endogeneity (via the tax function in this case). The budget surplus fails to separate the influence of the budget on the economy from the effects of the economy on the budget. One common, and popular, measure proposed to circumvent this problem is the cyclically adjusted or full-employment budget surplus:

$$dT(y^f, t) - dg \equiv T_t(y^f, t) dt - dg \tag{2}$$

where y^f is full-employment income. The cyclically adjusted deficit is an *ex ante* measure of stance in the sense that changes in fiscal stance, as captured in (2), will generate effects on income and expenditure through the operation of the multiplier. Shaw (1979) points out that the usefulness of the cyclically adjusted (or full-employment) deficit depends on whether fiscal policy changes the slope of the budget function. This can lead to misleading results. For example, an increase in the unemployment benefit rate will have little or no impact on the full-employment deficit but will have a large expansionary effect at lower levels of income. The financing implications of the cyclically adjusted deficit are usually ignored, and a more practical difficulty is the assumption of the underlying growth of productive potential required to calculate revenues at full employment. The NIESR have regularly published estimates of the full-employment deficit, for example Price (1978) and NIESR (1980), but such series are often subject to breaks as the assumptions regarding the growth of full-employment income are revised (often in an abrupt manner). The measure has also been used by Buiter and Miller (1983) in their (second) analysis of government policy under Mrs Thatcher. The models themselves do not generally produce an estimate of the cyclically adjusted deficit since full-employment income is normally undefined. The exception is the LPL model, where the cyclically adjusted deficit is used as a determinant of government expenditure.

One disadvantage of measuring fiscal stance by either the actual or cyclically adjusted surplus is that it treats all transactions as having equal impact. An alternative is to weight the various components of the surplus by their demand weights giving a standardized measure. The so-called demand-weighted or standardized surplus can be written in this case as

$$c'T_t dt - dg.$$

Like the cyclical adjustment, it represents only the impact effect of a change in fiscal policy; and, even more so than the cyclically adjusted measure, it is not 'model-free', in that knowledge of c' and T_t is needed. The weights themselves attempt to account for the differential incidence of private spending on different forms of revenue and expenditure. Blinder and Solow favour this measure because the expression above is simply the impact effect of fiscal policy on output, as can be seen from the solution of the fix-price *IS/LM* model for a local change of y:

$$dy = \frac{dg - T_t c' \, dt + c_r dm}{1 - c'(1 - T_y) + l_y c_r / l_r} \ .$$

The macroeconomic models themselves automatically allow for this weighting procedure but do not produce any summary *ex ante* measure. While there have been several attempts to measure fiscal policy stance through the various methods described above, comparable estimates for monetary policy stance are almost non-existent. A major reason for this is disagreement over which monetary policy variables are to be regarded as instruments.

Blinder and Solow conclude in their survey that there are no 'model-free' measures of policy stance. Although this provides a natural use for macroeconomic models, their very nature — being large, nonlinear, and dynamic — raises various problems with all of the measures outlined. In particular, they concentrate on income and not other macroeconomic variables. The interrelationship with other policy assumptions (monetary policy, incomes policy, etc.) are not included, and, more specifically, the implications of how the deficit is financed are ignored. The measures also give no guidance as to what the appropriate time response of the endogenous variables should be, usually concentrating on the impact effect. Finally, the impact of expectations on private sector activity is ignored, although this reflects the nature of the models themselves. These considerations have led Buiter (1984) to conclude that 'The "demand weighted" . . . cyclically corrected deficit . . . is the proper index of the short-run (first round) demand effects of fiscal policy only in a static, rather old-Keynesian and expectations innocent model.' The model above fits this description perfectly.

A more fundamental objection made by Buiter concerns the issue of sustainability of fiscal stance. This questions whether the deficit conveys any useful information relating to the net worth or permanent income of the public sector, two concepts central to this type of analysis. The conclusion is that the deficit contains little or no information on the *sustainability* of fiscal stance, or on the *consistency* of the long-term budgetary plans, and is uninformative as to the *credibility* of the government's budgetary, debt, and monetary policy. The issues of consistency and credibility are beyond the scope of this chapter, but sustainability has a bearing on interpreting the deficit as a measure of stance. The analysis (which summarizes the more detailed accounts of Buiter, 1983a,b; Miller, 1982; Miller and Babbs, 1983) is concerned with the precise determinants of the net worth of the public sector and its effect on fiscal and financial plans. Buiter defines a sustainable fiscal plan as one where the ratio of current real government consumption expenditure, $g(t)$, to the real public sector worth, $W'(t)$, at time t equals either (i) the short real interest rate, $i(t)$, net of the trend rate of growth of output, η, or (ii) the long real rate of interest, $I(t)$. The degree to which this ratio exceeds each of the interest rate measures defines, in turn, 'the constant net worth deficit', $D^w(t)$ and the 'permanent deficit', $D^p(t)$, given by

$$D^w(t) = g(t) - \{i(t) - \eta\} \, W'(t) \tag{3a}$$

$$D^p(t) = g(t) - I(t)W'(t). \tag{3b}$$

When either deficit is zero, the conditions for sustainability referred to above are satisfied. If it is true that these measures are a more meaningful concept than the deficit or PSBR, then Buiter argues that 'corrections' to the PSBR are necessary. He provides a list of such corrections and attempts to measure them, thereby providing historical estimates of the 'permanent deficit' PSBR (Buiter, 1984, Table 3). The degree of complexity in calculating these corrections and the use of data not normally found on the databanks of econometric models prohibit the models from providing such *ex post* measures. However, two particular corrections are of concern to at least two of the models.

The first correction, cyclical adjustment, has already been considered, but now the foregoing analysis provides us with a further justification for examining this issue. The adjustments are desirable not only because they provide a better approximation to the short-run demand effect of the budget, but also because they are a step towards the calculation of the net worth of the public sector.

The second correction is the inflation adjustment of the deficit, and it is within the scope of existing models to provide historical measures. Moreover, one particular model, LPL, determines private sector wealth explicitly, and this occurs as an argument in various functions, namely expenditures on durables, non-durables, and the demand for real-money balances. As private sector wealth represents a liability to the government in the LPL model, the inflation adjustment made in the LPL definition of wealth reflects the same in the measurement of the public sector net worth. At a very simple level, the adjustment reflects the need to revalue public sector debt interest payments at the real rate of interest rather than the nominal rate. The following simple model, taken from Miller (1982), explains why. Suppose that all public sector debt is issued in the form of Treasury bills, so that

$$DW = G - T' + rW \equiv PSFD \qquad (4)$$

where

W is the nominal value of public sector debt
G is the nominal public sector expenditure (excluding interest payments)
T' is public sector tax receipts in nominal terms
r is the nominal Treasury bill rate
$PSFD$ is the nominal public sector financial deficit
w is the real value of public sector debt, $w \equiv W/P$
P is an index of the price level
D is the first derivative operator, $DX \equiv dX/dt$.

Two so-called real measures of the deficit are distinguished:

(i) 'constant price' PSFD:

$$\frac{PSFD}{P} = \frac{G - T'}{P} + rw = \frac{DW}{P} \qquad (5)$$

(ii) 'inflation-adjusted' PSFD:

$$PSFD^{\dagger} = G - T' + (r - DP/P)W = DW - \frac{DP}{P}W. \qquad (6)$$

The latter computes debt interest payments at the real rate of interest rather than the nominal rate. The relationship between the two measures arises by subtracting (6) divided by P from (5):

$$\frac{PSFD}{P} = \frac{PSFD^{\dagger}}{price\ index} + \frac{adjustment\ for\ inflation}{price\ index}.$$

Equation (4) indicates that a zero PSFD maintains a constant level of *nominal* public sector debt. Now consider Dw:

$$Dw = D(W/P) = \frac{DW}{P} - \frac{DP}{P}\frac{W}{P} \qquad (7)$$

which is simply the right-hand side of (6) divided by P. This is the constant-price inflation-adjusted PSFD, and setting this measure to zero maintains the *real* value of outstanding debt at a constant level.

Miller (1982) produces estimates of the adjustment for inflation. The calculation is relatively straightforward: the market value of net liabilities of public corporations and general government (measuring W) is multiplied by inflation and subtracted from the published debt interest payments (measuring rW). This is compared with a similar estimate produced by the Bank of England (1982) and another example of the same calculation is provided in Buiter and Miller (1983). The calculation clearly requires one piece of information not normally found on the models' databanks, namely an estimate of W (the exception is LPL), although it is within the scope of the models to provide historical estimates of this adjustment.

5.3   Model-based policy measures

It is generally agreed that measures of policy stance are model-dependent, as was forcibly argued by Blinder and Solow (1974). This has led to the formal use of macroeconomic models to derive measures of policy on a counterfactual basis. This approach consists of simulating a macroeconomic model under a neutral assumption of fiscal and monetary policy and comparing the results with a model simulation based on actual historical values of the fiscal and monetary instruments. The difference between the solution trajectories (or the statistics describing them) is then the measure of policy impact. Blinder and Goldfeld (1976) used the MIT–Penn–SSRC (MPS) model of the US economy to examine the influence of monetary and fiscal policy on real GNP from 1958 to 1973. Applications of this method have been carried out in the UK, on various vintages of models, by Artis and Bladen-Hovell (1984), who use the NIESR model over the period 1979-82, Artis and Green (1982), who use the HMT model to examine the 1974-9 period, and Artis *et al.* (1984), who use both the HMT and NIESR models to measure policy over the period 1979-82. This methodology has also been used in the study commissioned by the Bank of England (1982) using the LBS and NIESR models to examine the factors underlying the 1980 recession.

The simulation approach has the advantage that demand weights are automatically incorporated in the calculations, and the models themselves allow for the dynamic effects of policy so that the overhang of policies from previous periods are recognized. It is therefore possible to derive a measure of fiscal and monetary policy period by period, and Artis *et al.* (1984) argue that, under approximate linearity of models, the contribution of the components of fiscal and monetary policy can be separately identified using an incremental approach.

Here the cumulative effects of policy are built up by simulating the models for each policy instrument one by one.

One particular problem arises in that no two models generate the same answers. Some of the studies referred to above attempt to allow for this by using two alternative models, but the 'true' answer is no more obvious when two different measures are obtained. Christodoulakis and van der Ploeg (1984) have addressed this problem by setting out a method that pools all the models.

Interpreting fiscal and monetary stance from counterfactual simulations is also dependent on prior views about their objectives. This is because model simulations produce not an estimate of policy stance itself but a set of differences in various endogenous variables, for example output, inflation, and employment. A set of weights is required so that a single index can be obtained, whose change measures whether the policy has been expansionary or not. (When only one variable is being considered, such as output in the simple fix-price *IS/LM* model above, this problem does not arise.) Now fiscal and monetary policy are set out in terms of effects rather than as a description of behaviour, that is, in terms of an *ex post* outcome rather than as *ex ante* stance. This clearly means that assumptions regarding other policies are critical in the base-run or neutral policy simulation. Estimation of fiscal policy stance is highly dependent on assumptions about the accompanying monetary policy. The importance of the financing assumption itself can be seen from simulations with the HMT model in Chapter 2.

Although most of the studies have been used to measure the past effects of policy, the same methodology can be applied to future policy assumptions. The problem then is that the effects depend on the exact set of instruments used.

Many of the assumptions used in Artis *et al.* (1984) to derive the neutral policy simulation originate from the Bank of England study (1982). These are an indexed tax system with public expenditure growing in line with trend output. Because transfer payments are not usually modelled in terms of rates, these are ignored. Monetary policy is defined as no change in the real rate of interest, and this is approximated by taking the actual difference from a given (nominal) constant minimum lending rate, and therefore ignores any impact on expected inflation from the policy change. The Lucas critique also hangs over all of these studies. This is explicitly discussed by Artis *et al.* (1984), who cite the possibility of a substantial regime change over the period 1979-82. In their analysis of this period Buiter and Miller (1983) note the major changes in stockbuilding, employment, and exchange rate relationships. A major problem concerns exchange rate policy. In some studies (e.g. Artis and Green, 1982) this is simply a constant exchange rate, whereas in others (e.g. Worswick and Budd, 1981) the exchange rate is allowed to adjust to preserve the level of price competitiveness. However, as in the relative assumptions between monetary and fiscal policy, the linkage between monetary and exchange rate policy is not made explicit. These relationships between monetary and fiscal policy are part of the model structure in that each fiscal policy change is always financed in a standard way, but the models vary considerably in this standard treatment; moreover, the explicit financing arrangements are often not clear. The following section expands on these issues.

5.4   The interrelationship between monetary and fiscal policy

One major criticism of the measures of fiscal policy outlined in the preceding sections is that the assumption regarding the financing of the deficit is not specified. Where monetary policy is explicitly set, as in the Bank of England study (1982) and Artis *et al.* (1984), this consists of a fairly *ad hoc* assumption about nominal interest rates rather than a formal account of the public sector's budget constraint. Our discussion of the financing issue is concerned with three main questions:

(i)   Is the identity explicitly modelled or implicitly assumed? If it is the former, what implications are there for the determination of the residual asset, namely bonds, via Walras' Law?

(ii) What assumptions are made about how the deficit is financed, that is, who is accumulating the counterpart of public sector debt, and how?

(iii) Is the public sector being modelled on its own, or is it being consolidated with the banking sector?

A useful reference point is the following standard textbook representation of the public sector budget constraint:

$$DM + DB + e\,DR = G(\cdot) - T'(\cdot) + rB - er^*R \equiv PSFD \qquad (8)$$

where

M is nominal stock of money
B is nominal stock of bonds
R is nominal stock of reserves
e is nominal domestic price of foreign currency
G is nominal public sector public expenditure and transfers
T' is nominal public sector public tax revenues
r is nominal domestic rate of interest
r^* is nominal foreign rate of interest

(Equation (8) generalizes (4) by introducing bonds and reserves.) Of course, textbook examples often overlook practical modelling issues, and several are discussed below. Of particular relevance is the exogeneity assumption. For example, in the LBS model the interest rate variable is endogenous, but it can be exogenized in order to be used as a policy instrument.

All of the models, with the exception of Liverpool, treat fiscal policy in a fairly standard way; namely, the deficit is set in nominal terms from assumptions made about tax rates and government spending. The models differ in the degree of detail with which the components of expenditure and taxation and other items of the public sector accounts are treated. We can think of the PSBR being made up of four different components: (i) current and capital expenditure ($P_g g$) and subsidies and transfers (T_0); (ii) tax revenues, being the product of a rate (t) and a nominal base (denoted Y, to capture the notion of nominal activity); (iii) financial transactions (G_k); and (iv) interest payments, W^r. Typically, g and t are exogenous with Y and P_g endogenous, the treatment of T_0 differing between models. The PSBR is not controlled directly since it depends on the nominal level of activity: fiscal stance is set by expenditure and tax rates. Consequently, the models reflect the endogeneity issues discussed earlier, through expenditure as well as receipts.

In the LPL model a constant-price version of the PSBR is determined as follows:

$$real\ PSBR = g - ty + w^r \qquad (9)$$

where y and w^r are deflated versions of Y and W^r referred to above. In contrast to the other models, real government expenditure is endogenously determined, 'an underlying level, g^*, is derived from the exogenous *PSBR* target, $PSBR^*$, and tax revenue net of debt interest; actual spending, g, varies around this in a counter-cyclical manner' (Minford *et al.*, 1984). Formally,

$$g/g^* = (y/y^*)^{\frac{1}{2}} \qquad (10)$$

$$g^* = ty^* - PSBR^* - w^r \qquad (11)$$

(* refers to long-run or target values). Output and its long-run level are determined in the rest of the model; there is an equation determining debt interest, w^r, which is different from the other models (a point to which we return later), and so the tax rate and $PSBR^*$ remain as the exogenous determinants of fiscal stance. In fact, in the actual model the exogenous instrument is $PSBR^*/y^*$. The tax rate, t, may be thought of as an implicit index of the relevant tax rates, two of which occur in the rest of the model, namely employers' and employees' tax rates on labour. An explicit link between these and t is not made. (Indeed, it is calculated by (9) given data on all the other variables.) The same point can be made concerning the unemployment benefit rate. However, LPL recognizes the endogeneity of government spending and transfers, as in (10), partly to capture the unemployment benefit payments component.

There is a greater contrast between the models in their explanation of the financing of the PSBR. The CUBS model follows the standard textbook treatment:

$$PSBR = (M - M_{-1}) + (B - B_{-1}) - (R - R_{-1}). \qquad (12)$$

The nominal stock of reserves, R, now denominated in domestic currency, is assumed exogenous. The nominal money stock is determined by another financing equation:

$$\ln M = \ln M_{-1} + \mu + D_1 (0.016 + B/B_{-1} - 1) \qquad (13)$$

where D_1 is a dummy whose value is zero up to 1986 and unity thereafter, and μ reflects the operation of the Medium-Term Financial Strategy. When $D_1 = 0$, μ defines the exogenous proportional growth in the nominal money stock, and (12) implicitly determines the quantity traded in the bonds market via Walras' Law. When $D_1 = 1$, μ is an exogenous policy instrument driving a further wedge between endogenous growth rates in money and bonds. This switch in financing at 1986, when the MTFS is no longer assumed to operate, has quite marked effects on the dynamic properties of the model, since any increase in the PSBR does not affect monetary growth and hence inflation before 1986, but has a major inflationary effect in the post-1986 period. In principle, the built-in assumptions regarding financing can be varied by changing values for μ or by changing the constant term (0.016). No interest rate variables exist in the CUBS model, so that a bond-financed expansion has no effect on the rest of the model. The operation of alternative financing arrangements would involve the rewriting of (13).

In the Liverpool model the financing of the deficit is given by one equation:

$$\frac{DM}{M} = k \left(\frac{PSBR}{y} \right)^* + 0.02 \qquad (14)$$

where $k = 2$. The assumptions are that 'money supply growth is determined by the long-run PSBR target converted to its equivalent growth in financial assets, plus a small allowance (0.02) for the differential growth in money because of its transactions role. We found no *systematic* cyclical behaviour of money supply in the floating period; hence non-underlying money growth is represented as random' (Minford *et al.*, 1984). Consequently there is an error term on (14) that is not shown. Notice that $PSBR^*/y^*$ determines both fiscal stance and how it is financed.

One of the motivations of this chapter is to examine whether the government's budget constraint is explicitly 'written down' in the models under consideration. The above equation is not such an identity; rather, it is a financing assumption. In the absence of the identity there is no explicit link between fiscal stance and the acquisition of public sector debt by either the private sector or the rest of the world. Put more succinctly, given an increase in fiscal stance by £1, there is no guarantee that the outstanding stock of government debt will increase by £1. As the stock of government debt held abroad does not enter the model, any differences between the decrease in the public sector's asset position and the increase in that of the private sector can be attributed to a change in the asset position of foreigners. Pure money expansion in the LPL model can be handled only by shocking the residual in (14) with the standard financing assumption, one of balanced growth in money and bonds.

The acquisition of private sector wealth is modelled explicitly, reflecting the role of this variable in various functions. In developing such an equation the public sector budget constraint *is* implicitly assumed together with the balance of payments on current account identity:

$$eDF + eDR = X + er^*(F + R) \tag{15}$$

where e is the domestic price of foreign currency. This identically relates the nominal current account surplus, X, to the net acquisition of foreign assets, $F + R$, by the private sector and public sector respectively and the interest income on the existing stock. Summing (15) and (8) yields the net acquisition of private sector wealth:

$$DM + DB + eDF = (G - T) + X + rB + er^*F. \tag{16}$$

(Notice that, if (15) is *assumed* to hold (there is no way of checking), then so must the government budget constraint.) The LPL model has an equation for the change in *real* private sector financial wealth, which we define as

$$A = \frac{M + B + eF}{P}.$$

Differentiating and substituting in (16) yields

$$DA = \frac{G - T}{P} + \frac{X}{P} + \frac{rB + er^*F}{P} + \frac{De \cdot F}{P} - A \frac{DP}{P}. \tag{17}$$

This simply states that the private sector acquisition of real wealth corresponds to the government deficit and the current account surplus (both in real terms), plus interest payments made on both domestic and foreign bonds (appropriately deflated), plus two other terms. These clearly are directly analogous to the inflation adjustments to the PSFD described earlier, except that here we are dealing with the private, not public, sector. The LPL model's version may be written as

$$A - A_{-1} \left\{ \frac{1 + 0.155(1 - Dr)}{1 + DP} \right\} = \frac{G - T}{P} + \frac{X}{P}.$$

The key differences between this and (17) are that the LPL definition of wealth does not contain foreign assets and revaluations of real foreign assets arising from depreciating or appreciating currency. This reflects the difficulty in measuring such a stock variable.

In the LBS model the money stock is determined by a reduced-form relationship which relates the stock of money to the PSBR, the net acquisition of financial assets by the industrial and commercial sector, interest rates, and the lagged stock of money. The short-term interest rate is dependent on the world rate with all the other short-term interest rates related to this rate in a simple manner. While some of these interest rate relationships are formally endogenous in the LBS model, they may be regarded as forecasting relationships, so that in policy exercises interest rates could be treated as policy instruments. It is not always clear, however, which of these relationships are useful forecasting rules rather than behavioural relationships.

Whereas CUBS define the measure of money as M0 and Liverpool as M_1 (see Figure 5.1), LBS use the more usual £M_3 definition. This has important implications for the discussion of the relationships between money and bonds. In the

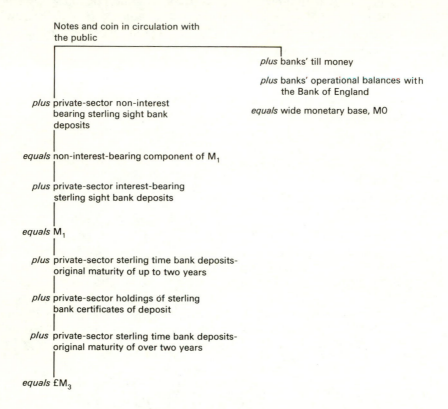

Fig. 5.1   Relationships among the monetary aggregates

CUBS model bonds are determined as the residual finance of the PSBR, while in the Liverpool model bonds are determined residually from the demand for real-money balances. One of the potential issues not explored further here is the implication of different definitions of money for the various treatments adopted, and in particular for the assumption of residual bond-financing. Bonds are the residual item in the LBS model but it is not possible to derive a simple expression for their determination.

In general, we can express the finance of the PSBR as

$$PSBR = NC + DEBT + EXT + BLPU$$

where

NC is increase in notes and coin
DEBT is sales of public sector debt to the UK private non-bank sector
EXT is external finance of the public sector
BLPU is increase in sterling lending to the public sector.

The increase in the $£M_3$ definition of money is given by

$$\Delta M = NC + BLPU + BLPR + BLOS - OSD - FC - NON$$

where

BLPR is increase in sterling lending to the UK private sector
BLOS is increase in sterling lending to overseas residents
OSD is increase in overseas sterling deposits
FC is increase in net foreign currency deposits
NON is increase in non-deposit liabilities.

Therefore the increase in $£M_3$ can be written as

$$\Delta M = PSBR - DEBT + BLPR + BLOS - EXT - OSD - FC - NON.$$

In familiar terms,

$$\Delta£M_3 = PSBR - gilt\ sales + increase\ in\ bank\ lending + net\ external\ flows$$
$$- increase\ in\ non\text{-}deposit\ liabilities.$$

Bank lending to the personal and company sectors are modelled explicitly in the LBS model, together with the demand for notes and coin, but as noted above, the overall PSBR/M_3 relationship is estimated rather than derived by identity. There is therefore no explicit relationship between money and bond financing of the PSBR. The PSBR/$£M_3$ relationship itself is nonlinear, and thus it is not possible to write down analytically the long-run partial coefficient between the PSBR and M_3. Using simulation techniques (see Table 5.1) we find that a temporary increase in the PSBR leads to a permanent increase in the change in the money stock, while a permanent increase in the PSBR leads to an increase in the change in the money stock which tends towards the increase in the PSBR in the long run.

Table 5.1 *LBS model: impact of £2 billion exogenous change in the PSBR on the money stock*

Quarter	($£$ million)	
	Temporary shock	Permanent shock
1	–	–
2	119	1019
3	113	1062
4	105	1104
8	84	1280
12	71	1475
16		1700

The question of whether the banking sector is modelled explicitly has implications for the determinacy of monetary policy. Where the banking sector is consolidated with the monetary authorities, the supply of money can be treated as an exogenous variable under the control of the authorities, as in the CUBS and Liverpool models. Where the banking sector is separated, the supply of money is partially endogenous, as the banks can vary their reserve asset ratios with interest rates being a key policy instrument. Bank lending is modelled explicitly in the LBS (and NIESR) models. But interest rates are formally endogenous in the LBS model, so that the only monetary policy instruments in the LBS model are minimum deposit rates on durables. Moreover, since the £M_3 equation is not a demand relationship, it cannot be inverted to characterize a situation of pure bond finance whose interest rates rise to keep the money stock constant.

The NIESR modelling of the monetary sector has some similarities to the LBS framework. It uses £M_3 as the measure of money and also separates out the banking sector. However, it differs in four main ways. First, it has a demand-for-money equation which determines the level of the M_1 measure of money. Second, the £M_3 measure of the money stock is determined by an identity; and third, the short-term interest rate is exogenous and can be treated as a policy variable. Finally, the demand for gilts is modelled explicitly. The NIESR model uses the following framework: from endogenous levels of the PSBR, gilt sales and demand for notes and coin, and exogenous levels of external transactions, the change in bank lending to the public sector is determined as a residual. Thus,

$$BLPU = PSBR - DEBT - NC - EXT.$$

From the identities described earlier ΔM can now be derived as:

$$\Delta M = BLPU + BLPR - NON + NC - OSD - FC + BLOS$$

where *BLPR* is endogenous and *NON* is non-deposit liabilities, which, together with external finance and net foreign currency transactions, are treated as exogenous. Thus there is no formal accounting link between the money stock and the exchange rate/balance of payments sectors. In the LBS model the exchange rate depends on the money stock, but the balance of payments does not enter the PSBR/M_3 relationship.

Unlike the LBS model, debt sales are modelled explicitly, depending on interest rates and stocks of financial assets held by the private sector. Since short-term interest rates are exogenous, simulations with the NIESR model involving an expansion in public expenditure correspond closely to the traditional money finance assumption. Bond finance would correspond to setting *BLPU* equal to zero, which in turn implies that interest rates rise to equate the PSBR with the increase in debt sales. However, attempts to simulate a bond-financed expansion, by a set of multiple runs, described by Brech (1983), have shown instrument instability, probably arising from the multiplicity of interest rates. The interest rate in the debt equation is the long rate (consol rate), which is related to the Treasury bill rate (the policy instrument) and inflation.

The model is not set up in a form whereby one can easily endogenize the Treasury bill rate to solve the debt equation.

The CGP have a full-blown model of financial stocks with a disaggregation of the private sector into six institutional groups. These stock models are determined by portfolio decisions, and the money stock (and bonds) are determined explicitly from the appropriate identities.

5.5 How useful are the models in answering questions about fiscal and monetary policy?

In the preceding sections we have outlined some of the main issues underlying the measurement of fiscal and monetary stance and described the monetary and fiscal framework of the models. We now examine the appropriateness of these models as vehicles for monetary and fiscal policy analysis.

Most of the measures of policy discussed in Section 5.2 are model-dependent. This is largely because measures of fiscal policy are *ex post* estimates of policy effects rather than *ex ante* estimates of plans. The fact that different models embody different views regarding the transmission effects of monetary and fiscal policy, and in turn their impact on the economy, means that general statements regarding fiscal and monetary influence cannot be made. (Not only are measures of fiscal stance model-dependent: they are also instrument-dependent.) In addition, differences in the financing assumptions between the models mean that different conclusions could be drawn from the same exercise conducted on different models even if their true monetary and fiscal responses were identical. In Section 5.4 we have argued further that, not only is the treatment of deficit finance not standard across models, but it is not easily modified within each model, so that in many cases it is not possible to examine how relevant the financing assumption is. One model that is not discussed in detail, the HM Treasury model, does not suffer from this disadvantage, and simulation results from the HMT model (see Chapter 2) reveal that the choice of financing is important. The reason why the HMT model can deal with alternative financing arrangements is the incorporation of a demand-for-money function that can be inverted, but this is not a necessary condition for such flexibility. It is not of course impossible in principle for the proprietors of these models to operate them in an environment that achieves the desired financing result (e.g. through an optimization approach). However, the publicly available versions of these models described here cannot vary the financing assumption unless the user is very sophisticated in the use of the model, and even then the appropriate adjustments must be rather *ad hoc*. This implies that such issues as crowding-out cannot be tackled consistently with current models and available software.

In Section 5.4 we noted that the definition of money varies between the models. This limits comparability exercises between models. It implies that even identical financing assumptions do not generate the same impact. For example, the general use of residual bond financing means that time deposits would be

Table 5.2 *Monetary and fiscal policy instruments*

Fiscal policy instruments		Monetary policy instruments	Definition of money	Financing arrangements
Expenditure	Revenue			
LBS				
Current expenditure on procurement and employment Non-housing capital expenditure (general govt and public corporations) Housing capital expenditure (real) Transfers (real) Subsidies (real) Unemployment benefit rate	Income tax rate and allowances VAT rates (luxury, standard, petrol) Inflation adjustment to direct & indirect taxes Specific duty rates Nat. insurance surcharge rate Nat. insurance contribution rate	Minimum deposit on durables	$£M_3$	Reduced-form relationship between PSBR and $£M_3$
NIESR				
Current expenditure Capital expenditure (housing and non-housing) Current grants (money terms)	Income tax rate Corporation tax rate North Sea oil tax rate Nat. insurance contribution rate Employees' contribution rate Employers' contribution rate Tax rate on consumers' expenditure Tax rate on other final demand	Interest rates	$£M_3$	Identity between PSBR and $£M_3$
CGP				
Current expenditure (5 groups) Capital expenditure (5 groups)	Income tax rate Tax allowance VAT rate Corporation tax rate North Sea oil taxes Inflation adjustment to taxes Nat. insurance surcharge rate	Interest rates	$£M_3$	Endogenous financing depends on wealth and interest rates through a portfolio model

	Specific duties Employers' contribution Employees' contribution			
CUBS Expenditure growth rate current and capital (both annual and cumulative) Unemployment benefit rate	Income tax rate Income tax allowances (real) VAT rate Employees' contribution rate Employers' tax rate North Sea oil tax rate	Money growth (to 1986)	MO	Money exogenous to 1986, then PSBR financed by fixed proportion of money and bonds
LPL Unemployment benefit rate	Income tax rate Employee tax rate Employers' tax rate	PSBR/GDP ratio	M_1	Balanced portfolio between money and bonds

counted as bonds under a LPL model simulation but as money in the NIESR or LBS models. Nor can the models be used outside of a policy-optimization environment to examine the relative merits of the exchange rate–money supply target debate. In the LPL model all fiscal and monetary policy measures are fully anticipated and allowed for in current behaviour, whereas the other models ignore announcement and expectations effects, making no distinction between anticipated and unanticipated measures. (In the HM Treasury model manual some of the simulations involving expenditure and tax changes assume that the lag response of certain variables is altered by the change in policy, but these adjustments are made subjectively and imposed on the model.)

An examination of Table 5.2, which provides a summary picture of the fiscal and monetary instruments in each model, reveals a paucity of monetary policy instruments. In several cases there is no independent monetary policy variable and monetary growth can be varied only through fiscal policy in conjunction with the assumed financing rule. This is a further illustration of the difficulty in assessing monetary policy independently of fiscal policy.

In contrast to the lack of monetary policy instruments defined by the models, there is a plethora of fiscal policy instruments. Even so, there are certain basic questions that cannot easily be answered. One of these concerns the calculations of the balanced-budget multiplier or the effect of pure fiscal policy. Government expenditure is generally set in volume terms and with the tax assumption being one of tax rates, so that the implied money expenditure and revenue effects (*ex ante*) are not explicit and require some prior calculations. The Liverpool model comes close to allowing the operation of a balanced budget effect by exogenizing the PSBR–GDP ratio. In the other models the PSBR is treated as an identity and cannot be exogenized under present practice.

The fact that the input assumptions for government expenditure are in constant price terms means that the money cost of expenditure is endogenous. Thus, most of the models cannot simulate the effects of a cash limit expenditure policy. An exception is the CGP model, where this option is available in addition to the standard volume of expenditure assumption. As with some of the other issues noted earlier, the models could in principle incorporate this feature as an option, but this requires some additional relationships to those already identified.

The list of fiscal policy instruments in Table 5.2 also suggests where some models are more appropriate than others for examination of certain issues. For example, the LBS model is the only one to distinguish between procurement and employment expenditure, while the CGP model disaggregates expenditure by functional category. Whereas the LBS separates out public corporations' capital expenditure from that of general government, the LPL model combines current and capital expenditure and treats them as endogenous.

On indirect taxes the LBS and CGP models can vary the inflation adjustment factor to specific duties while the disaggregated nature of the CGP model enables it to select the indirect tax rate by type of tax (or subsidy) rate on any of 42 commodities as an instrument. In the NIESR model full inflation indexing is automatically assumed, while specific duties are not identified in the CUBS and LPL models. Nor does the LPL model distinguish the rate of VAT, but in contrast LBS and CGP specify both the standard rate and differential rates.

The comments on indexing of indirect taxes also apply in general to the indexing of income tax allowances with the principal exception of CUBS, who specify the tax allowance in real terms. All the models distinguish the rate of income tax as a fiscal policy instrument but only CGP and NIESR include the corporate tax rate. CUBS, LPL, and CGP distinguish between employer and employee taxes, and NIESR between the national insurance (NI) contribution rate and employers' contribution, whereas the LBS has one NI contribution rate. LBS and CGP distinguish separately the national insurance surcharge.

The absence of a North Sea sector from the LPL model means that it is unable to answer questions about the taxation of this sector. The other models all include North Sea taxation variables, but the absence of any links between North Sea taxation and productive activity and investment mean that the impact of changes in this variable are solely on tax revenue. Government transfer payments are set in constant price expenditure terms in the CGP model (where they are disaggregated) and LBS model and in current price terms in the NIESR model. The unemployment benefit rate is distinguished in the CUBS and LPL (and also in LBS) models, but no other transfer payments appear as a fiscal instrument.

A final, but by no means minor, point concerning the relevance of the macro-economic models to monetary and fiscal policy measurement is that of policy reaction. In contrast to the practice adopted in forecasting, where it appears that some implicit policy optimization may be taking place (see Chapter 3), the models typically do not incorporate policy reaction effects. Exceptions are in the NIESR model, where the exchange rate equation incorporates an interest rate reaction effect, and in the LPL model, where government spending is endogenized. While the lack of policy reaction may illustrate some interesting features about the models themselves, it is a potential disadvantage in policy analysis.

5.6 Summary and conclusions

In this chapter we have examined some of the issues involved in measuring fiscal and monetary policy stance and the ease with which the models can be used for policy exercises. One general conclusion is that there is no independent measure of fiscal or monetary policy stance in the models and that attempts to satisfy some predetermined stance are highly instrument-dependent. An illustration of this is given in Chapter 3, which shows that a similar broad policy background (the MTFS) is interpreted in different ways by the model teams. A further finding is that the relationship between monetary and fiscal policy is often ill-defined and non-standard across the models. This implies not only that cross-model comparisons are potentially misleading, but also that the use of an individual model for a given policy exercise may be inappropriate. To some extent the problem arises from the lack of an explicit budget constraint in the models. Yet another problem arises from the different measures of money and the consequent difficulty in interpretation of the assumptions about the finance of a given deficit.

The lack of monetary policy instruments in the models poses problems for research on the effects of monetary policy. In most of the models monetary effects arise through the setting of fiscal policy and this prevents examination of an independent role of monetary policy.

Finally, we note that, although the models can answer some fairly standard questions about the objectives of fiscal policy, there are many others that cannot be answered easily by the outside user of the model. There are also some major differences in what sort of questions can be answered by which models. Some of these are the result of a different general approach to modelling and therefore a legitimate product of the modelling activity, but others represent more of a difference in detailed treatment which does not have this rationale.

References

Altonji, J.G. and Ashenfelter, O. (1980). Wage movements and the labour market equilibrium hypothesis. *Economica,* **47**, 217–245.

Andrews, M.J. (1983). The aggregate labour market – an empirical investigation into market clearing. London School of Economics, Centre for Labour Economics, Discussion Paper no. 154.

Andrews, M.J. and Nickell, S.J. (1982). Unemployment in the UK since the war. *Review of Economic Studies,* **49**, 731–759.

Artis, M.J. (1972). Fiscal policy for stabilization. In *The Labour Government's Economic Record, 1964–70* (W. Beckerman, ed.), pp. 262–299. London: Duckworth.

Artis, M.J. (1982). Why do forecasts differ? Paper presented to the Panel of Academic Consultants, no. 17, Bank of England.

Artis, M.J. and Bladen-Hovell, R.C. (1984). Monetarist macroeconomics in practice: the first Thatcher government 1979–82. *Socialist Economic Review* (forthcoming).

Artis, M.J., Bladen-Hovell, R.C., Karakitsos, E. and Dwolatzky, B. (1984). The effects of economic policy 1979–82. *National Institute Economic Review,* no. 108, 54–67.

Artis, M.J. and Green, C.J. (1982). Using the Treasury model to measure the impact of fiscal policy, 1974–79. In *Demand Management, Supply Constraints and Inflation* (M.J. Artis, C.J. Green, D. Leslie and G.W. Smith, eds), pp. 30–47. Manchester: University Press.

Ball, R.J. and St Cyr, E.B.A. (1966). Short-term employment functions in British manufacturing industry. *Review of Economic Studies,* **33**, 179–197.

Bank of England (1982). Inflation-adjusted saving and sectoral balances. *Bank of England Quarterly Bulletin,* **22**, 241–242.

Barber, J. (ed.) (1984). HM Treasury macroeconomic model: Supplement to the 1982 technical manual. Government Economic Service Working Paper no. 71.

Barker, T.S. (ed.) (1976). *Economic Structure and Policy.* London: Chapman and Hall.

Beenstock, M., Warburton, P., Lewington, P. and Mavromatis, T. (1983). A medium-term macroeconometric model of the UK economy 1952–1982. Working Paper, City University Business School.

Blinder, A.S. and Goldfeld, S.M. (1976). New measures of monetary and fiscal policy, 1958–1973. *American Economic Review,* **66**, 780–796.

Blinder, A.S. and Solow, R.M. (1974). Analytical foundations of fiscal policy. In *Economics of Public Finance* (A.S. Blinder *et al.*), pp. 3–115. Washington DC: Brookings Institution.

Brech, M. (1983). Comparative structures and properties of five macroeconomic models of the UK. National Economic Development Office Working Paper no. 10.

Brechling, F. (1965). The relationship between output and employment in British manufacturing industries. *Review of Economic Studies,* **32**, 187–216.

Britton, A. (ed.) (1983). *Employment, Output and Inflation: The National Institute Model of the British Economy.* London: Heinemann.

Buiter, W.H. (1983a). Measurement of public sector deficit and its implications for policy evaluation and design. *IMF Staff Papers,* **30**, 307–349.

Buiter, W.H. (1983b). The theory of optimum deficits and debt. London School of Economics, Centre for Labour Economics, Discussion Paper no. 177.

Buiter, W.H. (1984). Allocative and stabilization aspects of budgetary and financial policy. Inaugural Lecture, London School of Economics.

Buiter, W.H. and Miller, M.H. (1983). Changing the rules: Economic consequences of the Thatcher regime. *Brookings Papers on Economic Activity*, 1983, no. 2, 305–365.

Capella, P. and Ormerod, P.A. (1982). Earnings and the pressure of demand in the UK. Economist Intelligence Unit, Working Paper no. 402.

Christodoulakis, N. and van der Ploeg, F. (1984). Macro-dynamic policy formulation with conflicting views of the economy. Unpublished paper, University of Cambridge.

Desai, M., Keil, M. and Wadhwani, S. (1983). Incomes policy in a political business cycle environment: A structural model for the UK economy 1961–80. London School of Economics, Centre for Labour Economics, Working Paper no. 167.

Fisher, P. and Salmon, M. (1984). On evaluating the importance of nonlinearity in large macroeconometric models. ESRC Macroeconomic Modelling Bureau Discussion Paper no. 2.

Foster, N., Henry, S.G.B. and Trinder, C. (1984). Public and private sector pay: A partly disaggregated study. *National Institute Economic Review*, no. 107, 63–73.

Friedman, M. (1968). The role of monetary policy. *American Economic Review*, 58, 1–17.

Greenhalgh, C. and Mayhew, K. (1981). Labour supply in Great Britain: Theory and evidence. In *The Economics of the Labour Market* (Z. Hornstein, J. Grice and A. Webb, eds), pp. 41–66. London: HMSO.

Hall, S., Henry, S.G.B. and Trinder, C. (1983). Wages and prices. In Britton (1983), pp. 65–78.

Hazeltine, T. (1981). Employment functions and the demand for labour in the short run. In *The Economics of the Labour Market* (Z. Hornstein, J. Grice and A. Webb, eds), pp. 149–151. London: HMSO.

Hansen, B. (1970). Excess demand, unemployment, vacancies and wages. *Quarterly Journal of Economics*, 84, 1–23.

Henry, S.G.B. (1981). Forecasting employment and unemployment. In *The Economics of the Labour Market* (Z. Hornstein, J. Grice and A. Webb, eds), pp. 283–309. London: HMSO.

Henry, S.G.B. and Ormerod, P.A. (1978). Incomes policy and wage inflation: empirical evidence for the UK, 1961–1977. *National Institute Economic Review*, no. 85, 31–39.

Henry, S.G.B., Sawyer, M.C. and Smith, P. (1976). Models of inflation in the UK: An evaluation. *National Institute Economic Review*, no. 77, 60–71.

Hilton, K. and Heathfield, D.F. (eds) (1970). *The Econometric Study of the United Kingdom*. London: Macmillan.

Holden, K., Peel, D.A., and Thompson, J.L. (1982). *Modelling the UK Economy*. Oxford: Martin Robertson.

Holly, S., Rustem, B. and Zarrop, M.B. (eds) (1979). *Optimal Control for Econometric Models*. London: Macmillan.

Howrey, E.P., Klein, L.R. and McCarthy, M.D. (1974). Notes on testing the predictive performance of econometric models. *International Economic Review*, 15, 366–383.

Klein, L.R. (1979). Use of econometric models in the policy process. In Ormerod (1979), pp. 309–329.

Klein, L.R., Ball, R.J., Hazelwood, A. and Vandome, P. (1961). *An Econometric Model of the United Kingdom*. Oxford: University Press.

Kooiman, P. and Kloek, T. (1979). Aggregation of micro-labour markets in disequilibrium: Theory and application to the Dutch labour market 1948–1975. Econometric Institute, Erasmus University, working paper.

Lawson, T. (1981). Incomes policy and the real-wage resistance hypothesis: Econometric evidence for the UK, 1955-1979. Cambridge Growth Project, Paper no. 509.

Lucas, R.E. and Rapping, L.A. (1969). Real wages, employment and inflation. *Journal of Political Economy*, 77, 721-754.

Miller, M.H. (1982). Inflation-adjusting the public sector financial deficit. In *The 1982 Budget* (J. Kay, ed.). Oxford: Basil Blackwell.

Miller, M.H. and Babbs, S. (1983). The true cost of debt service and the public sector financial deficit. Unpublished paper, University of Warwick.

Minford, A.P.L. (1983). Labour market equilibrium in an open economy. *Oxford Economic Papers*, 35 (Supplement), 207-244.

Minford, A.P.L., Marwaha, S., Matthews, K. and Sprague, A. (1984). The Liverpool macroeconomic model of the United Kingdom. *Economic Modelling*, 1, 24-62.

Minford, A.P.L. and Peel, D.A. (1983). *Rational Expectations and the New Macroeconomics*. Oxford: Martin Robertson.

Mortensen, D.T. (1970). A theory of wage and employment dynamics. In *Microeconomic Foundations of Employment and Inflation Theory* (E.S. Phelps et al.). London: Macmillan.

Muellbauer, J. (1978). Macrotheory vs macroeconometrics: The treatment of 'disequilibrium' in macromodels. Birkbeck College, Discussion Paper no. 29.

Muellbauer, J. and Winter, D. (1980). Unemployment, employment, and exports in British manufacturing: A non-clearing markets approach. *European Economic Review*, 13, 383-409.

National Institute of Economic and Social Research (1980). The economy in 1979. *National Institute Economic Review*, no. 91, 10-13.

Nickell, S.J. (1980). Some disequilibrium labour market models: Further formalization of a Muellbauer type analysis. London School of Economics, Centre for Labour Economics, Working Paper no. 205.

Nickell, S.J. (1981). An investigation of the determinants of manufacturing employment in the UK. London School of Economics, Centre for Labour Economics, Discussion Paper no. 105.

Nickell, S.J. (1983). Working hours in Britain. London School of Economics, Centre for Labour Economics, Working Paper No. 565.

Nickell, S.J. (1984). A review of 'Unemployment: cause and cure', by Patrick Minford, with David Davies, Michael Peel, and Alison Sprague. London School of Economics, Centre for Labour Economics, Discussion Paper no. 185.

Nickell, S.J. and Andrews, M.J. (1983). Unions, real wages and employment in Britain 1951-79. *Oxford Economic Papers*, 35 (Supplement), 183-206.

Ormerod, P. (ed.) (1979). *Economic Modelling*. London: Heinemann.

Osborn, D.R. and Teal, F. (1979). An assessment and comparison of two NIESR econometric model forecasts. *National Institute Economic Review*, no. 88, 50-62.

Peterson, W. (1982). Employment and productivity. Paper presented at Cambridge Growth Project Conference, Jesus College, Cambridge.

Phelps, E.S. (1967). Phillips curves, expectations of inflation and optimal unemployment over time. *Economica*, 34, 254-281.

Phelps, E.S. (1970). Money wage dynamics and labour market equilibrium. In *Micro-economic Foundations of Employment and Inflation Theory* (E.S. Phelps *et al.*). London: Macmillan.

Posner, M.V. (ed.) (1978). *Demand Management*. London: Heinemann.

Price, R.W.R. (1978). Budgetary policy. In *British Economic Policy* (F.T. Blackaby, ed.). pp. 262–279. Cambridge: University Press.

Renton, G.A. (ed.) (1975). *Modelling the Economy*. London: Heinemann.

Sargan, J.D. (1964). Wages and prices in the United Kingdom: A study in econometric methodology. In *Econometric Analysis for National Economic Planning* (P.E. Hart, G. Mills, and J.K. Whitaker, eds), pp. 25–54. London: Butterworth. Reprinted in *Econometrics and Quantitative Economics* (D.F. Hendry and K.F. Wallis, eds), Blackwell, 1984.

Sargan, J.D. (1980). A model of wage-price inflation. *Review of Economic Studies*, **47**, 97–112.

Sargent, T.J. (1978). Estimation of dynamic labour demand schedules under rational expectations. *Journal of Political Economy*, **86**, 1009–1044.

Sargent, T.J. (1979). *Macroeconomic Theory*. New York: Academic Press.

Savage, D. (1983). The use of the model for forecasting. In Britton (1983), pp. 111–120.

Shaw, G.K. (1979). The measurement of fiscal influence. In *Current Issues of Fiscal Policy* (S.T. Cook and P.M. Jackson, eds), pp. 44–60. Oxford: Martin Robertson.

Symons, J.S.V. (1982). Relative prices and the demand for labour in British manufacturing. London School of Economics, Centre for Labour Economics, Discussion Paper no. 137.

Thirlwall, A.P. (1983). What are the estimates of the natural rate of unemployment measuring? *Oxford Bulletin of Economics and Statistics*, **45**, 173–175.

Tinsley, P. (1971). A variable adjustment model of labor demand. *International Economic Review*, **12**, 482–316.

Wadwhani, S.B. (1982). Wage inflation in the UK. London School of Economics, Centre for Labour Economics, Discussion Paper no. 132.

Wallis, K.F. (1971). Wages, prices and incomes policies: some comments. *Economica*, **38**, 304–310.

Wallis, K.F. (1979). *Topics in Applied Econometrics* (2nd ed.). Oxford: Basil Blackwell.

Whitley, J.D. (1983). Incomes policy in aggregate wage equations: Some suggestions for modelling. Institute for Employment Research, Discussion Paper no. 25.

Worswick, G.D.N. and Blackaby, F.T. (eds) (1974). *The Medium Term: Models of the British Economy*. London: Heinemann.

Worswick, G.D.N. and Budd, A.P. (1981). Factors underlying the recent recession. Paper presented to the Panel of Academic Consultants, no. 15, Bank of England.

Wren-Lewis, S. (1982). A model of private sector earnings behaviour. Government Economic Service Working Paper no. 57.

Wren-Lewis, S. (1983). Employment. In Britton (1983), pp. 52–64.